ACCLAIM FOR *BRAZEN CAREERIST*

"This book has the street smarts you need to make your career and life work for you from the start. Read it now, or you'll wish you had when you're forty!"

—KEITH FERRAZZI, BESTSELLING AUTHOR OF
NEVER EAT ALONE: AND OTHER SECRETS TO SUCCESS, ONE RELATIONSHIP AT A TIME

"A road map to help navigate corporate life...Trunk's style is direct, practical, and anecdotal, and most important, incredibly helpful."

—JULIE JANSEN,
AUTHOR OF *I DON'T KNOW WHAT I WANT, BUT I KNOW IT'S NOT THIS*

"There are two kinds of people in the workplace: *careerists* and *achievers*. If you've been too busy achieving to focus on how to move your career forward, this book is a must read. It will teach you how to find just the right balance between the two."

—DR. LOIS P. FRANKEL, *NEW YORK TIMES* BESTSELLING AUTHOR OF
NICE GIRLS DON'T GET THE CORNER OFFICE

"Trunk brings considerable savvy and a fresh new perspective to the business of career success. Bold and sometimes unconventional, BRAZEN CAREERIST gives readers much to think about as well as concrete, practical suggestions that will help them know what they want and know how to get it."

—PAUL D. TIEGER, COAUTHOR OF *DO WHAT YOU ARE* AND CEO, SpeedReading People, LLC

"This book is the *What Color Is Your Parachute?* for the new generation."

—BRUCE TULGAN, AUTHOR OF *MANAGING GENERATION X*

BRAZEN CAREERIST

THE NEW RULES FOR

SUCCESS

PENELOPE TRUNK

WARNER
BUSINESS
BOOKS ™

New York   Boston

Warner Business Books
Hachette Book Group USA
237 Park Avenue
New York, NY 10169
Visit our Web site at www.HachetteBookGroupUSA.com.

Warner Business Books is an imprint of Warner Books.
Warner Business Books is a trademark of Time Warner Inc. or an
affiliated company.
Used under license by Hachette Book Group USA, which is not
affiliated with Time Warner Inc.
Printed in the United States of America

First Edition: May 2007

10 9 8 7 6 5 4 3 2 1

Library of Congress Cataloging-in-Publication Data
Trunk, Penelope.
Brazen Careerist: the new rules for success / Penelope Trunk.
p. cm.
Includes index.
ISBN-13: 978-0-446-57864-6
ISBN-10: 0-446-57864-9
1. Career development. 2. Vocational guidance. 3. Success in business.
I. Title.
HF5381.T736 2007
650.1—dc22
2006027623

Acknowledgments

My agent, Susan Rabiner, saw all my weaknesses within three minutes of first meeting me, which made life with her great because there was nothing I could hide. She has encouraged me in all aspects of life, and she has taught me how to follow the rules while at the same time inspiring me to succeed in unorthodox ways.

I would be lying if I told you that writing a book was easy. My editor, Diana Baroni, transformed me from a columnist to an author. No small feat. Sometimes I imagine that while she was going through edits with me on the phone, she was throwing darts at a wall to keep her voice so even. Leila Porteous saw me through rocky moments, and Jamie Raab and Rick Wolff believed in this book even when I wished it was a book but it wasn't.

I am a writer who loves a good editor. So I am thankful to a slew of editors who have helped me along the way. The easiest lesson was from Jessica Pompei: to just be myself. The hardest lesson was from Daniel Ray: to follow the rules. Jim Krusoe made me believe I was a writer and taught me not to write about writing. Leslie Epstein accepted me into grad school and accepted that I was not grad school material. Susanna Kaysen fed me rice at night while I spent my days as a starving grad student. Tim Carvell encouraged me to nag people until I got a column. Ned Desmond and Josh Macht gave me my first column, and Josh taught me to never write about my sex life in a business magazine. Riza Cruz taught me that I am more interesting when I am useful. David Wallis taught me to stop worrying about the last column and focus on the one I am writing. Perri Capell was my editor and then my networking project, but she also turned out to be a friend. Caleb Solomon gave me a chance to write for the *Boston Globe*. Doreen Vigue taught me to pay attention to pictures. Andrew Caffrey taught me the value of editorial banter. Tanya Singer gave me the opportunity to write for Yahoo! Hundreds of other editors have run my syndicated column in print and online, and this broad editorial enthusiasm has allowed me to keep writing.

My husband has been flexible with his own life so that I could go after my dreams, no matter what they were. He stayed up late teaching me HTML so that I could run a Fortune 500 Web site (yes, that's all it took in 1994). He managed a long-distance relationship so I could continue to run my company. He encouraged me when I took an 80 percent pay cut to be a full-time writer. He took care of our kids so I could finish my book.

Finally, I want to thank the people who have read my column and my blog. Some have been reading since 1999. Some have just started. Everyone who has written to me has taught me something. I write about careers because I love the dialogue about what we can do to find happiness in work and life. I hope this book continues that dialogue.

Contents

Introduction

Every generation is known for something. My generation is revolutionizing work. Today there are new rules, new expectations, and new standards for success. If, like me, you are a member of Generation X or Y, that is, between the ages of eighteen and forty, this book will help you make good decisions so that you can get an exciting, rewarding career that helps you grow and accommodates your personal life.

As an older member of Generation X, I found myself constantly out of step with coworkers at the beginning of my career. I did not value the same things they did, I did not want their lives, I did not want their jobs—I wanted something different. After ten years in the workforce, I realized that I wasn't weird for expecting my job to be fun (and for being disappointed when it wasn't). I wasn't lazy for moving back home with my parents. I was actually part of a large trend, but when you're helping start a trend, often you look less like a trendsetter and more like a freak.

I wrote this book to provide a road map that I wish I'd had when I started out in business. This isn't a book by a career coach, advising you on how to navigate a world she never had to navigate. These are firsthand stories and practical advice on how our generation can successfully maneuver in the new workplace, from someone who's been there.

Here are some characteristics of the new generation of workers that set us apart from those who came before us:

- We move back with parents after college: In 2005 65 percent of college seniors planned to move back home.
- Career instability is a given and we hold more than eight jobs before age thirty-two.
- We invented the quarterlife crisis in which career and relationship problems come to a boiling point at around age thirty.
- Women don't aspire to be Superwomen; in fact, five years after business school, only 60 percent of women are working outside the home.
- We demand control and flexibility when it comes to work, which explains why 40 percent of all new businesses are started by people under thirty-four.

These new workers are forcing revolutionary changes in corporate life, and these changes will occur on magnitudes we have not seen since women entered the all-male office.

Work will become more fun, more fulfilling, and more accommodating of a personal life in the next five years. This revolution is due to the seemingly outrageous expectations of young people—and their already apparent ability to get them met. One of the biggest topics in management consulting right now is how to change corporate life in order to retain young workers, because they won't stay if they don't like what's happening.

But don't mistake Generations X and Y for lazy. We are passionate, hardworking, and devoted to our friends and family. We are ambitious, we work hard to be inclusive and to make the world a better place, and we have an unparalleled ability to make things in our lives happen fast.

So we need new rules and new guidelines for success. The old discussion about workplace issues is quickly becoming irrelevant because we are seeing the end of work as we—and our bosses—know it:

The end of gender-based pay disparity. Today, pay is equal for men and women until they have kids. But this inequality will change when Generation Y starts having kids, because the men of that generation are committed to being equal partners in child rearing and are choosing low-stress jobs from the start of their careers. Young men today are prepared to trade power and money for time at home with their children.

The end of the glass ceiling. It will end not because women will finally make it into the top ranks of the Fortune 500 in significant numbers, but because most women will stop caring. And so will men.

Generations X and Y will give up a lot to achieve balance in work and life—something the older generations were not willing to do. So advice like "Don't leave gaps in your resume" is simply unsupportive and unrealistic. Young people need to cope with inevitable gaps in clever, new ways.

The end of the grind. More and more people will choose a career because they love what they do. People will want to work to be part of something larger than themselves and as a path to personal growth. People will choose a career as a way to keep the job of raising children from becoming dull and alienating.

The end of consulting. All workers will feel like consultants, so the term will be useless. Employers will decrease costs by encouraging consulting rather than long-term, salaried employment in the office. Employees will push for this to get more flexible hours. This is not a large leap given that younger workers already feel no long-term loyalty and tend to be project-focused instead of job-focused.

The end of the stay-at-home parent. Both men and women will look for flexible jobs that accommodate child rearing. Many younger women have already rejected the idea of sacrificing time with their children to a relentless, high-powered, long-houred job, and men are following suit. The most fulfilled moms tend to be those with a flexible job that accommodates young kids in a way that doesn't make the mom crazy with guilt or stress. Like women, men who plan to stay at home with kids actually plan to work part-time, too.

So the question "Should you be a stay-at-home mom?" is not all that useful to the men and women of this generation, first, because it is gender-specific, and second, because it is too black and white. A more relevant discussion is how to plan for shared parenting and flexible work to accommodate raising children.

The end of hierarchy. Pecking order really only matters if you are working at the office all day, reinforcing ranks. So the less time people spend at their desks, the less they will care about rank. Young people have no interest in climbing ladders when they know they probably won't be working at one place long enough to hit every rung.

The classic career topic of "How to Get a Promotion" will become irrelevant. That's not what today's employees are after. The younger generation of workers cares more about personal development and honing job skills they can take with them to their next job or career.

The new workplace emerges at a time when psychologists are just starting to quantify what, exactly, makes people happy. The new worker will respond to this data quickly: Happiness Studies 101 is the most popular course among Harvard undergrads, and the research is infiltrating every discipline imaginable. Here's a sample of the research: you only need $40,000 to be happy; after that, what impacts your happiness the most is your personal relationships. So ladder-climbing advice like "pay your dues" does not ring true to workers who believe money doesn't matter that much. What young people are looking for is advice about how to get interesting work without giving up a personal life.

If you recognize yourself in this new workplace, then this book is for you. If you don't feel that the old, typical rules of business should apply, then the advice in this book is for you. This book will advise you on how to be successful at work, knowing full well that the definition of success has changed radically so the rules have to change, too. The advice in this book would not have applied to the workplace fifteen years ago. Tips like *Use harassment to boost your career, Differentiate yourself by staring at the wall,* and *Make a strategic move to your mom's house* all provide tactics to get what you want from a career in the twenty-first century.

This book is for a generation that asks for more from their work than anyone has asked for in history—a generation that is making new roadmaps for new careers. This is a guide to getting the things that the current generation cares about from a generation that doesn't understand that. This book is about achieving success on new terms.

My own work life has unfolded in a way similar to many workers in the new generation: I was lost. But then I learned how to get what I wanted from my boss and I used these new rules to make adjustments to fit both my personal and professional lives.

My resume depicts a successful marketing executive, serial entrepreneur, and widely read business columnist. But my story began in the sand, as a professional beach volleyball player. I spent three years training twelve hours a day to get to the beach tour. I worked insane jobs that accommodated beach hours, and I often went hungry when rent was due.

When I reached the upper echelons of the sport, I realized that the skill that made me stand out most on the professional beach volleyball tour was not my jump serve but my ability to market myself to sponsors.

After failed attempts at hijacking my boyfriend's marketing business and at graduate school, I found my place in the software industry in Southern California. I rose through the ranks fast. I had a knack for writing and for office politics—a lethal combination that allowed me to land plum assignments, enlist the aid of top workers, and then write scintillating reports to highlight my successes. I sailed through Fortune 500 companies, startups, an IPO, and a merger.

Then I had the good fortune to work for a CEO who gave me seed funding for a new company. After the startup phase, I sold my shares of the company and I started another, which exploded at the same time as the Internet bubble.

Proving that failure is necessary for success, soon after that, Time Warner asked me to write a weekly column about my life as an executive in corporate America. The column, Brazen Careerist, which still runs today, had ironic timing: I was unemployed, single, strapped for cash, and, for the most part, lost. I worried about revealing too much about my plight in the column, but it turned out that I was documenting a journey through a quarterlife crisis before there was a name for it, and the column gained a huge readership.

As a serial career changer who has had many business roles in many different fields, I relied heavily on books to guide me through my personal reinvention. But I never saw a broad-sweeping career handbook with proven advice that specifically reflected the experience of my generation back to me. So I wrote this one.

The chapters in this book are based on my own experience and the career advice columns I've written for the new generation of workers for publications such as the *Boston Globe, Business 2.0* magazine, and USATODAY.com, as well as advice I've gathered from successful young business people and a wide variety of experts. Many people who pop up in the chapters are those whom I've met through work during the past fifteen years, as well as friends and family who now know better than to tell me anything they don't want to see in print.

Part One covers the first stages of a twenty-first-century career: being lost, figuring out the type of career that's right for you, and marketing yourself to get the job you want. This section lays out options—grad school, the job search, entrepreneurship, travel—and helps you evaluate which are best for you. I'll show you how to feel good about making decisions for yourself in a world where there is not necessarily a right decision. Lastly, Part One introduces you to the idea that there are scientifically proven rules for how to find a career that's right for you and how to be happy, and you can follow them, easily, for great results.

Part Two helps you get what you want from your boss. This part of the book is for people who know what they want but are having a hard time getting it. You'll find advice to help guide you if you feel impatient with your current job situation; if you have great ideas and your boss keeps shooting them down; or if you work with people who drive you nuts. These tips will help you stick to what you value while maneuvering around corporate roadblocks and annoying personalities that get in your way.

Along the way you'll also find advice on how to protect your personal life from the demands of work. You must start planning early in order to position yourself to have synergy between your work and your home. This book is for visionaries who are changing the world one worker and one family at a time. It's also for people who are already at the stage of their life when balance is imperative, but they don't yet have it; these tips will help you see a new workplace with new possibilities that were not there even five years ago.

For Generations X and Y work is not just a means of support, but a lifestyle choice that must challenge, entertain, and encourage personal growth. But the current workplace is not set up to offer this sort of work to young people, so you will have to maneuver strategically within a baby-boomer-dominated workplace to attain goals that are unique to a new generation. This book outlines the new rules for success and provides tactical moves to ensure that you get the kind of work you want without getting derailed by outdated ideas of what work should be.

BRAZEN
CAREERIST

I

Relish the Path from Starter Job to Dream Job

When I graduated college I was being recruited by a publishing house in New York. During the interview I asked where people play beach volleyball in Manhattan. Insane, I know. Subconsciously I was sabotaging my interview because I really wanted to be able to play on the beach. So what was I left with after that interview? No job offer from the publishing house, a string of other jobs that didn't matter to me, and wild dreams of being a professional athlete.

At night, when I was alone, I panicked that I would never find a way to support myself. I worried that I was risking everything for a volleyball dream that might never pay off. I wondered if I was looking like a loser—but I wasn't worried enough to get a job mindlessly shuffling paper from nine to five.

One of the contributions Generations X and Y have made to the workplace is the quarterlife crisis. It's not the midlife crisis, typified by a baby boomer in a Porsche obsessively speeding. The quarterlife crisis happens in a person's late twenties and more likely involves takeout pizza and obsessive IM-ing.

The journey toward quarterlife crisis begins at college graduation, when the typical student has about $20,000 in loans, no skills to land a job, and no money to pay sky-high rents in the cities where being single is the most fun. With little to lose, most twentysomethings use their postcollege time as an opportunity to find themselves, see what's available, and try a lot on for size (which translates to 8.6 jobs before the age of thirty-two, according to the Department of Labor).

In fact, this new behavior pattern, which looks remarkably like flailing, is a great idea for the new workplace. This is the time in life when people should try out their dreams, many of which will entail living in poverty with no health insurance. Not that that's good. But better to do it now than when you're forty.

This is the time to snoop into other people's lives. Take a look at what makes other people happy and try it out. Notice who is looking like their life stinks, and stay away from the choices they've made. Navigating the workplace from college to the quarterlife crisis is the process of testing your dreams and passions and figuring out where you will fit.

Job-hopping in your early twenties is a great idea— especially if you're still sleeping at your parents' house. After all, the point of this period in life is to find the *right* work for you. But if the job-hopping doesn't stop by age thirty, the feeling of instability intensifies to crisis. Young people want work to be a learning experience and consistent with their values and lifestyle choice, which can make a job search difficult.

This is true for Alexandra Robbins. She took the first job offered to her after college because she was seduced by the trappings: short commute, friends at the company, office with a door. "The pay was fine," she said, "but the work was not rewarding."

Alexandra, twenty-eight, realized that in the post-college world, people are judged by their answer to the question, "So, what do you do?" And she knew she needed to have an answer she was proud of.

Alexandra understands that previous generations were more equipped to make the transition to adulthood. "Our generation cannot gain a foothold in society until age thirty. But our parents' generation has age twenty in their head. The crisis is a clash of generations." Fifty years ago, people expected to find a job for life right after college and be married with kids by age twenty-four. But for the current generation, Robbins declares, "Thirty is the new twenty."

The problems start at around age twenty-seven or twenty-eight, when most people find a career. For those who do not feel settled, there is panic and what Jeffrey Arnett, author of *Emerging Adulthood: The Winding Road from Late Teens through the Twenties,* calls "desperate and dangerous" measures—such as quitting a job and not having any savings—in order to reach their goals: hence, the quarterlife crises.

The key to becoming settled before you hit a crisis is to invest time in getting to know yourself. Try a lot of paths, meet a lot of people, and figure out what you're good at. This is a process of trial and error and there is no substitute for taking risks and living with uncertainty. But there is a reward: you will construct a life that integrates friends, family, and passions, and you will have a career that reflects deep thought and years of experimentation.

Part One will show you how to lay the groundwork for this life and avoid the quarterlife crisis. You will find relieving justification for not knowing what you want to do and inventive paths to take in order to figure out and begin a career that's right for you. You'll learn how to approach the job hunt like a direct mail campaign, how to ace your upcoming job interview, and whether you might be an entrepreneur in hiding. I will show you how giving a full passport more weight than a full wallet will set you on the way to a career you love.

CHAPTER ONE

Detours Are the Route to Happiness

One of the best decisions you can make in your twenties is to explore. Exploring postcollege options looks a lot like being lost; in fact, being lost is normal and productive at this stage in life. "I tell students there is no rush here. Career interests typically don't solidify until about the age of twenty-five. All the research shows that," said Linda Arra, director of career services at Lafayette College.

At earlier points in life, people are penalized for getting lost. For example, dropping out of high school for a year to explore makes colleges think you were hospitalized for mental instability. But it's a different story right after college: you don't get dinged for taking time off. "Most graduate and professional schools today would prefer the students take time to go away, have different experiences, and then come back refocused," said Bill Wright-Swadel, director of career services at Harvard College.

Part of the reason there is so much institutional respect for exploration is that there is no better way of figuring out what will make you happy. "We are not very good at using our imaginations when it comes to how we'll feel in a given circumstance," says Daniel Gilbert, a professor of psychology at Harvard University who specializes in figuring out what makes people happy. Therefore Gilbert recommends that we test out a lot of different careers. He admits that this tactic takes time, but he says it's worth it because otherwise you're likely to make a decision based on money, which, research shows, is not likely to have much impact on your happiness.

What about the people who pull their life together in a tight little package by age twenty-four? They're the exception to the rule, according to Wayne Osgood, professor of sociology at Pennsylvania State University. He labels these people "fast starters" and explains that they are only about 12 percent of the population. This group typically does not finish college and appears to have conventional personalities and the same expectations as their parents' generation. Some fast starters are just plain lucky: they love the first job they get after college. The other 88 percent of us have to trudge through our twenties formulating a new career plan.

The good news is that this is what most people *are* doing in their twenties: wandering. Taking trips to Thailand, changing jobs every year, volunteering for unpaid work while living at their parents' house, and starting businesses that fail. All these options are, surprisingly, right on track for making a good decision about what to do with yourself in adult life.

1. BE A SPONGE

There are lots of paths to happiness and most of them include an annoying job or maybe even ten. The most important thing about an annoying job is that you make sure you are learning and growing. Before you throw a fit and leave, consider that the most successful people are curious, with a broad range of interests, and can learn from anyone.

I spent the majority of my twenties doing jobs that raised eyebrows—as in "Are you a loser?" But I learned a lot from each job I had because any job—really, *any* job— can help your career if you let it. Each person, no matter how weird, has something to teach you. And each business has a gem of genius because, hey, they're making enough money to pay you, aren't they?

Some of the best negotiating training I got was from a job I had on a French chicken farm. I only took the job because I had a deal with the family who owned it: I would perform household chores in exchange for room and board (in France). To me, "chores" meant sweeping and dusting. To them, it meant killing and plucking chickens. In my lame French, I told the matron of the house that killing animals was not among my duties. She said I'd be kicked out for breaking the agreement. So I learned to pluck. Lesson #1: *Get all your agreements in writing.*

It was important to move the chickens into the buyer's truck before they realized what was happening. So in the middle of the night, while they were sleeping, we grabbed the chickens by the legs and held them upside down. The farmer couldn't believe I did it without throwing up. Immediately I asked for three days off and got them. Lesson #2: *Timing is everything when you ask for a concession.*

I picked cherries from the branches that were too high for the eight-year-old daughter who was also doing chores. Later she gathered the eggs out from under the hens so I wouldn't get pecked. Lesson #3: *Everything in life is open to negotiation because everyone has something they can give you.*

Relatives of the host family came to visit from Lyon. I had more in common with the city French than the rural French did. They invited me to stay with them in the city so their kids could learn English: another job offer! And the farmer overheard. So I told the farmer I would stay to harvest the hay only if I didn't have to feed the pigs anymore. Lesson #4: *Get a job offer in your hand to get more leverage at the job you have.*

The truth is that negotiating skills apply to every situation, and the worse shape you're in, the more essential the skills are. Had I not been suffering with the animals I probably wouldn't have paid so close attention to how to negotiate a break.

At another point in my life my friend got me a job signing Esther Williams's autograph for fans. In the 1940s and '50s Esther was a star of MGM water musicals: think Ginger Rogers with nose plugs.

I hated the job because I felt like I was wasting my time. I thought of myself as a misplaced generator of big ideas. But in hindsight I'd have to say that Esther Williams was my first marketing mentor, and later I built my own marketing career around rules I learned from lame tasks I did while working for her.

During my first week, Esther gave me three copies of her signature (different pens, different sizes) and told me to practice. I submitted my best shot to Esther and she said, "Make the E's loopier." I looped and resubmitted and then she gave me the go-ahead. Lesson #5: *Quality assurance is part of marketing—you can't brand something that is inconsistent.*

We had stacks of old MGM promotional photos in which she looks like a showgirl. But for the die-hard fans who requested it, I also had a headshot photo of Esther when she was about fifty years old. Lesson #6: *Give the customers what they want.*

We had 8×10s, but I only sent those if the person enclosed postage. Otherwise, Esther instructed me to send a 5×7. Sometimes people would request an 8×10, and even if they didn't send postage, I'd send a big photo. I figured it would make a happy customer and it wouldn't break Esther's bank—after all, she was still receiving residual checks from *Million Dollar Mermaid*. Lesson #7: *Know when to follow rules and when to use your own judgment.*

At the time I didn't understand that Esther Williams had spent a lifetime cultivating her own brand. I was lucky to see the intricacies of maintaining the brand, even if the operation was a little eccentric.

I realize now that the reason I picked up so much information about negotiating and marketing from these less-than-challenging jobs is because those are areas that interest me. I'm good at them and I like watching how other people do it. You will notice in your early, random jobs that you gravitate toward certain lessons. What you like learning about is probably what you like to do. Learn from yourself by watching how you learn from others.

So if you find yourself in a job in which you're not learning anything, ask yourself whose fault that is. You can't stay at a dead-end job forever, but don't ever assume there's nothing to learn. The first step is to figure out what interests you most about the job, and then watch very carefully and ask a lot of questions.

2. UNCERTAINTY IS A GOOD GIFT WITH BAD WRAPPING PAPER

If you could see a movie of your life before you lived it, would you want to live it? Probably not. The thrill of living is that you don't know what's coming. In other words, uncertainty is what makes our lives fun.

Sure, it's hard to see uncertainty in such a positive light when you're out of work, or when you feel like you're flailing. But uncertainty is really another word for opportunity, and you can't harness an opportunity until you recognize it's there.

When Allison graduated from Harvard, she had opportunities all over the place and no idea what she wanted to do. She took a job in consulting but she knew she wouldn't stay there. She took the GRE and scored so high that she was able to supplement her income by tutoring students at Stanley Kaplan. Still, she didn't think she wanted to go to graduate school. Allison knew she wasn't doing what she wanted, but she didn't know *what* she wanted.

She worried. All her friends were going to graduate school or starting their own businesses. She was lost and panicking that she would never figure anything out. She wasn't even living in a city she planned to stay in, but she couldn't figure out where to go.

After six years, reality set in. Many of her friends who went directly to professional school had crises when they graduated because they weren't sure if they had picked the right profession. And Allison, by going with the flow and having a general plan in mind, got married, moved to the

Midwest, and leveraged her consulting experience to get a great position at a foundation she is very happy with and where her job is to dole out money to nonprofits.

In hindsight, Allison realizes that her years spent being lost were actually just a period during which she was finding her way: time well spent, and time we must all take if we're being honest with ourselves.

The only way to lead an interesting life is to encounter uncertainty and make a choice. Otherwise your life is not your own—it is a path someone else has chosen. Moments of uncertainty are when you create your life, when you become who you are.

Uncertainty usually begins with a job hunt, but it doesn't end there. Every new role we take on means another round of instability. Instead of fearing it, here are some new approaches to dealing with uncertainty:

Accept uncertainty instead of fighting it. Some of you work for unstable companies, or hold tenuous positions at stable companies, or have no idea where you will go next. If you can focus in the face of instability, you are more likely to be able to leverage opportunity.

The best way to focus is to gain a better understanding of what you want and what you can control in order to achieve your goal. Maybe you don't know exactly what you want, but no one ever has all the information they need. Paul Stevens trains career coaches and one of the topics he spends the most time on is how to teach people to deal with uncertainty in their career. "The more information you have, the more you realize you don't know. The key is to accept this, but not be paralyzed by it. Not knowing for certain opens opportunities for new knowledge, new career options, being free to invent your own career future."

You should be focused and flexible about what you want for yourself. "Treat your career goals as a hypothesis and balance time spent achieving your goals with time spent discovering them," advises Stevens.

Prepare for uncertainty. The most extreme example of this preparation is in Pema Chödrön's writings on accepting uncertainty (see, for example, *Comfortable with Uncertainty: 108 Teachings on Cultivating Fearlessness and Compassion*). Chödrön, a Tibetan monk who lives in Canada, recommends that people spend their lives coping with uncertainty—through meditation, yoga, and self-knowledge, preferably at a monastery. Probably you will not do this, but you can follow her advice in principle: face the fact that uncertainty is difficult and that you are at least a little anxious. As Chödrön would say, just be with that, since you can't change it.

Most of us will not have honed meditation as a coping tool, but there are other tools that can help you when instability hits your career. Building a network, saving money, being very good at something, and continuing to learn— these are all ways you can make yourself more prepared for uncertain times because you'll have more flexibility in your approach to dealing with instability.

Use uncertainty to make yourself shine. For those of you who have no idea what to do next in your life, remember that uncertainty is what allows you to surprise yourself.

If you could see each future step along the way, you'd never get the chance to be amazed at what you can do.

When I graduated from college, I went on to play professional beach volleyball. At the time I worried that the decision was crazy and that I wouldn't make the cut, but in the face of massive instability, beach volleyball seemed like a reasonable choice. Now it is one of the parts of my life I am most proud of.

Create uncertainty. Some of you are stuck in your career. The only way to get unstuck is to create instability. Say to yourself, "Maybe I can change my approach, maybe I can find a new specialty." In the face of a mortgage or a waning 401(k), creating instability seems absurd. But think of it another way: uncertainty is really another word for opportunity, and each of us should take responsibility for creating our own opportunities.

If you can see your life in front of you, you've got a problem. If you know what's coming, then you probably won't need to grow to deal with it. If you can see everything coming, then what is the challenge? You're on autopilot. And who wants that for a life? So embrace instability. This is where you make your life your own.

3. GRAD SCHOOL WILL NOT SAVE YOU

Whether you're thinking of a top-tier MBA or a PhD in anthropology, there is a right way and a wrong way to approach graduate school. You need to understand your dreams and what is required to achieve them. Also, you need to understand the marketplace and what it values.

If you dream of climbing ladders in the Fortune 500, John Challenger, CEO of the placement firm Challenger, Gray, and Christmas, advises you to get an MBA. "In today's environment a graduate degree is as important as a college degree a generation ago." And get it in your twenties when the degree can get you a better starting job. "Where you start is very important for where you end up."

But think twice before cashing in your chips for a less-respected school. Challenger says, "Top business schools have a premium value. If you attend the third tier, do it at night because the financial loss and career stagnation while you're in school do not outweigh the benefit of the degree."

For some people, though, graduate school is not so much a way to fulfill a dream as a way to put off finding one. We spend eighteen years in school being told what to do and being rewarded for meeting other people's goals for us. The adult world requires us to set our own goals and this is something school does not teach.

Much of the flight to graduate school is a result of grade inflation and fragile egos, says Thomas Benton, a pseudonym for an assistant professor who writes a column for the *Chronicle of Higher Learning*: "Humanities majors are used to being praised by professors. Many recent grads return to school when they discover that not everyone thinks they are as great as their humanities teachers did. Humanities don't have the objective standards of business. Going back to grad school allows people to reestablish their ego. But it is short lived because they have to face the same market when they get out."

Keep in mind that instead of making you more creative, MFA programs make you more qualified to teach. And the academic job market is extremely competitive. Take, for example, English literature: only one out of five people who enter PhD programs will get a job in that field. The rest will find themselves back at square one, waiting tables, albeit with improved literary banter, and looking for a career.

Lost humanities students with an eye for cash and stability often enter law school because other professional schools require too much math or science. Yet the land of lost lawyers is full, too, which confirms that if you don't have a passion for what you are going to learn in graduate school, you shouldn't go.

Jane Sommer, interim director of the career development office at Smith College, has heard all the bad reasons for going to graduate school and has some advice:

1. Try other jobs first. The people who do best in graduate school are those who find decent alternatives first and still want to go back to school.

2. Determine if an advanced degree is necessary. Talk to people who are where you want to be in ten years. Ask them if they needed a diploma to get

where they are. If they say, "I didn't get a diploma, these are the steps I took…," you can do those steps, too.

3. Don't bother using graduate school to wait out a bad economy. Chances are the one you're in right now is not particularly bad for job hunters.

4. IF YOU'RE STUCK, TAKE AN ADVENTURE

If you're out of work, or if your job is so annoying that you wish you were out of work, then it's time to take an adventure. It's important to take adventures during the time when you have very little responsibility. With no one to take care of but yourself, an adventure is a way to bolster your skills and your resume without suffering through another dead-end job.

In your next job interview, you'll need a good answer when someone asks, "So, what have you been doing?" You don't want to sound like you are withering, uninteresting, or watching television at your mom and dad's house, even if you are. Travel is a fine answer to this interview question. It's true, and you seem worldly. Traveling does teach you a lot.

The older, very gainfully employed sector of society looks at these adventures as an expensive, childish way to avoid reality. This is partly true, but who cares? The reality of adulthood is hard. There are no teachers stroking your ego with As, and there are no parents making sure you're doing fun and challenging activities every afternoon. So it is no surprise that putting off adulthood is appealing. In fact, taking an adventure to see how other people live is a good first step into adulthood.

There are some great things you can accomplish while you're adventuring:

You can use an adventure as a way to hedge your bets. Robert Buckley was a health-care consultant and hated it. He decided to quit and try to get work as an actor. But he had no experience acting, and he was too scared to try it without having a plan B. So he decided that after six months, if he got no nibbles from agents, he'd go to Japan to teach English while he figured out what to do next. (Happy ending: he got acting jobs.)

You can sort out personal problems. A lot of career issues are actually personal issues. Do I really want to be a doctor or am I just doing it to please my parents? Do I want to move closer to my boyfriend or am I happy where I am? These are issues that dictate your career choices but that cannot be solved by changing jobs or rewriting your resume. Putting yourself in a new situation, away from the outside influences you are used to, will help you get a more clear perspective.

You can learn what you don't want. When I worked on the chicken farm, one day we spent three hours looking for mushrooms in the forest. I said, "Why do we have to keep looking? It's taking so long and it's only mushrooms. Let's go home." The father said, "But how will we have wild mushrooms for salad?" I couldn't believe it. I wanted to have my mom buy some at the grocery store and send them via airmail. This is when I knew that although I thought living and working close to the land would be appealing to me, it wasn't. To me, it actually felt monotonous and intellectually dissatisfying.

There are a few ways to get the money to travel. The most obvious is that you should alter your lifestyle. Prolific travel blogger Ali Watters has a few suggestions:

- Don't get a car or a mortgage unless you absolutely need one.

- Give up smoking or expensive trips to coffee shops—it wastes money each day.
- Stay away from material possessions. Before each purchase, ask yourself what you'll do with it while you're traveling.

Ali also recommends that you travel somewhere cheap; a month in Europe will cost you three times as much as a month in Southeast Asia.

If Ali's advice is too hard to swallow, you might try lining up a job that's an adventure. If you are under thirty years old, you can benefit from reciprocal work agreements that the United States has with the United Kingdom, Australia, and New Zealand.

If you want to travel to other places, or if you're older than thirty, there's still hope for finding work. The creative, entrepreneurial spirit that is often squashed in a beginner can thrive in an adventure. For example, Sarah Baer founded a nonprofit with about $1,000 so she could get papers to spend a year helping natural disaster victims in Asia. Ann Armony quit her job as a nanny but she didn't have enough money for an adventure, so she got a job for the summer working at the South Pole. It's a barren town of about 300 people, and "summer," really, is no word for the place, but she loved the change of pace.

The bottom line about adventure is that there's little difference between a good entry-level job and an adventure. Both are about learning, trying new things, and making sure you don't starve. So when you are looking at your job choices, put travel right up there, on top with everything else. It's good for your resume and good for your life.

CHAPTER TWO

A Resume Is a Sales Tool, Not a Work Summary

Resume writing is a creative exercise that combines the skills of direct mail with the skills of a storyteller. You can be great at your job, but unless your current boss is going to personally arrange your next job interview, you're going to have to depend on your resume. Your resume gets you the interview, and you can't get a job without that.

At least during the job hunt, your resume becomes more important than what you've done in your career, because a bad resume can make a good career look bad (and vice versa). Take time to understand your own story—once you nail that down, you may learn a thing or two about yourself and be ready when you land the interview.

Here's how hiring works. Someone is in charge of sifting through a pile of resumes. If you answer an ad, your resume is somewhere between the middle and the bottom of the pile. If your mom plays tennis with the hiring manager's boss, then your resume is on top of the pile. The hiring manager looks through the resumes as fast as possible, trying to find candidates to interview. Each resume gets approximately ten seconds' worth of consideration.

You need to make sure you use those ten seconds to your best advantage. Every line of your resume must say you are amazing because you don't know where the person's eye will go first (though you can be sure the person won't read every line).

This chapter will show you how to manage those ten seconds most effectively. You'll learn to think of yourself as a direct mail writer instead of a job hunter. You'll learn the rules of resume writing, and you'll also learn the perils of sticking to them so closely that they undermine your ability to market yourself.

This might sound like a lot of work, but one way to gauge how seriously you are taking your career is by how much work you're willing to put into your resume.

5. WHEN YOU BREAK RESUME RULES YOU LOOK LIKE YOU DON'T KNOW THEM

Part of getting a job is conveying the idea that you will adhere to the business conventions that matter to whomever is hiring you. And even if you don't believe in these conventions, you need to fake it enough to at least get in the door for an interview.

So here are the resume rules you need to follow. Before you read them, promise yourself that you will not be defensive and proclaim that you are an exception to the rules. You are not. The rules are there so hiring managers can compare apples to apples. It makes their job easier. Even if you are an orange, you need to make yourself an apple to get hired: think of yourself as an apple with an orange tint, but you must be an apple.

One page. That's it. I don't care if you are the smartest person on earth or if you have founded six companies and sold each of them for $10 million. The point of a resume is to get you an interview, not a job.

When someone is sorting through a huge pile of resumes, they are not looking at second pages. So if you have something great on the second page, put it on the first. Then you will have nothing great on the second page and you will be able to get rid of it.

If you still think you need a longer resume, give someone one page of your resume and have them look at it for ten seconds. Ask them what they remember; it won't be much. They are not going to remember any more information in ten seconds if you give them two pages to look at; ten seconds is ten seconds.

People with resumes that exceed one page say, "I couldn't get it down to a page." But here's what a two-page resume says about you: "No ability to see the big picture." You are so mired in the details of your career that you don't know how to summarize it. This does not bode well for future career success. Cut your resume to one page.

No paragraphs. I shouldn't even have to list this rule because no one should still be using paragraphs on a resume. But recent grads do it all the time. In fact, the woman who edits my Web site, and who is definitely very smart, showed me her resume and I nearly died: all paragraphs.

No hiring manager reads paragraphs. With a stack of 500 resumes in front of her, she's scanning—looking for something that stands out enough to warrant an interview. Nothing stands out in a paragraph. So by using them, you take yourself out of the running unless the hiring manager is your dad's best friend and has no choice but to read your entire resume.

But here's a side-tip for you paragraph-writers: you are not big-picture thinkers. If you were, you would not even consider using paragraphs. You are a detail-oriented person. A flair for detail does not justify a resume with paragraphs, but while you are deleting them, you can take solace in the fact that you've learned something about yourself.

List achievements. This is the hardest rule to follow. You must list achievements, not job duties. Every line must quantify success. Anyone can do a job, but achievements show you did the job well. Past performance is the best indicator of future performance, so don't let someone think you just showed up for your last job and didn't succeed.

Since a resume is not about what you did but what you accomplished, don't write: "Managed two people and created a tracking system for marketing." Write: "Managed the team that built a tracking system to decrease marketing costs 10 percent." Most college graduates can do what employers tell them to. Not everyone will do it well. Think of it as the difference between writing "I went to my classes and took tests" versus "I have a 3.5 GPA."

I know what you're going to say next: "I can't quantify my success. I didn't have those kinds of jobs." You're wrong. Everyone has successes they can quantify.

Let's say you had a four-hour-a-week babysitting job, which I hope not very many of you will have to put on your resume. But for the sake of argument, let's say you took care of two kids. You could write: "Managed household in parents' absence and helped kids to raise their grades one letter." Stupid, yes, but you need to make even stupid jobs sound like marginal accomplishments.

Ditch the line about references on request. It's implied. Of course if someone wants a reference, you will give one. No one presumes that you will not. So when you include that line, you seem to not understand how the game is played. (Bonus tip: If you have an excellent reference, like a CEO of a Fortune 500 company who vacations with your parents, have the reference call right after you send the resume. This sets the tone for the employer to think you are amazing.)

Be a keyword-focused applicant. Only 3 to 5 percent of job seekers find employment through online job sites. In order to be in this small percentage, you need to tailor your resume to keyword searches. "Sending a resume to a big company's Web site is like sending your resume into a black hole," says John Sullivan, a human resources consultant and professor of management at San Francisco State University. "In a big company, your resume is sorted by an applicant tracking system."

These companies receive thousands of resumes a month and the tracking system sorts them by skill. Sullivan tells of a study in which researchers wrote one hundred perfect resumes for a specific job opening. Then the researchers added 10 percent more information to the resumes. Of those resumes, only 12 percent were picked up by the tracking system as qualified. This means that even when you are the perfect candidate, if you submit your resume blindly to a large company, there is an almost 90 percent chance that no human will ever see it. But you can increase your chances by knowing how to use keywords in your resume. "Recruiters locate individuals based on a certain skill set of the job they are looking to fill," says recruiting adviser Matt Millunchick. Try to imagine how someone else would use a search box to find qualified applicants, and be very specific about your skills on your resume.

These rules remain true if you post your resume to an online database. The masses of resumes on job sites are so unruly that human resources departments are paying people in India twenty dollars an hour to sort through to find the good ones, according to David Hanley, owner of Recruti'n. Therefore, even in this case, keywords are your best friends.

Tread lightly on the personal interests line. Your personal interests are not there to make you look interesting. They are there to get you an interview. Every line on your resume is there to get you an interview. So only list personal interests that reveal a quality that will help you meet the employer's needs.

If you are in sports marketing, then by all means, list that you kayak. If you were an Olympic athlete, put it down because it shows focus and achievement. If you are a mediocre hobbyist, leave it off. Personal interests that don't make you stand out as an achiever do not help you. And personal interests that are weird make you look weird, and you don't know if that's what your interviewer likes, so leave it off the resume.

Don't be a designer unless you are one. If you have more than three fonts on your resume and you're not a designer, I can promise you that you've botched the layout. Fancy fonts make people question your intelligence, according to Daniel Oppenheimer, professor of psychology at Princeton University. If design were easy, no one would get paid for it. Recognize your strengths and keep design elements to the bare minimum. And please, save Photoshop for cards to your mom: just because you know how to use the shading tools doesn't mean you know how to use them well.

The good news about resume rules is that they are, for the most part, egalitarian—anyone in any job can follow them. And since you won't have to reinvent a resume style for yourself, the rules actually make your life a little easier.

6. WHEN WRITING YOUR RESUME DON'T BE TOO HONEST

A well-written resume to one person is a pack of lies to another. Make sure yours falls somewhere in between, which is no small feat. We all know there is such a thing as stretching the truth too much. But there is also such a thing as being too honest.

My twenty-one-year-old brother, Erik, worked summers at Blockbuster Video where, predictably, none of the mostly teenaged employees followed company rules. In a fit of productivity my brother rearranged the displays to be in line with the standards sent from company headquarters. At the same time, store sales increased 10 percent. So (as the family resume writer) I wrote on his resume, "Assumed responsibility for in-store marketing and increased sales 10 percent."

At a family dinner, we passed around Erik's resume. (Yes, we do this in our family.) My thirty-four-year-old brother, Mike, said, "Are you kidding me? This is such crap. No one will believe this."

Erik kept that line in his resume, and he explained and supported it well when challenged in interviews. He landed a job at an investment bank.

Some lies, though, are not in the gray area. Some lies are just plain lies. And if you have a big one on your resume, you need to clean it up. For example, maybe you say on your resume that you worked at IBM for two years, but really you only worked there for one and spent a year job hunting and making Web pages for your mom's bridge group. In this case, you need to tell the truth about IBM: one year.

But you don't have to leave a yearlong gap. Be creative. Call yourself a project manager for the year you had no job. You can learn about yourself as you rework your resume—maybe you didn't think of yourself as a project manager, but actually you were.

When it comes to massaging the truth, no two people have the same limits. You need to be very clear on your own limits so you can stay within them. But be honest with yourself. Some people are very, very truthful on their resumes, and then, when they don't get hired, complain that everyone else is lying and life isn't fair.

It's not true that everyone else is lying. The people who get the most job offers are those who know how to package themselves. Figuring out how to do this is a lot harder than just spewing facts onto a piece of paper. If you are not packaging yourself, it's not because you are more honest than the next person, it's because you are more lazy.

Packaging yourself takes a lot of time. Turning each bullet into an achievement is very difficult. And asking for help is difficult. Instead of pretending you are morally above that, recognize that you are competing in a marketplace and marketplaces require marketing.

So do some serious work on your resume. Make sure that it is not so honest that you look like a loser and not so dishonest that you're going to be fired soon after being hired.

7. A COVER LETTER IS A PIECE OF DIRECT MAIL

Most cover letters are addressed to people you don't know, so let's just stop referring to them as cover letters since they are really sales letters. You are trying to sell yourself—to a stranger.

The best way to think about this letter is in terms of direct mail, so pay attention to the well-funded, unsolicited offers you find in your mailbox. Many of those envelopes have been created by the finest writers in the direct mail business.

Here are eight rules from direct-mail experts that should guide your cover letter writing.

1. Open with a bang. This is the line I used to write: "I am writing to apply for the position you advertised blah blah blah." But *duh,* of course you are writing to get a job. Why else does anyone write a cover letter? So use your first line to sell yourself and make yourself stand out. For example, "I think your company can use my exceptional sales skills and ten years of experience in your industry."

2. Don't waste other people's time. Your cover letter is the introduction to your resume. If your cover letter is longer than a page, then it is likely longer than your resume. And who ever heard of an introduction that is longer than the main event? Also, write a separate letter for each job because each sentence of your cover letter should be specifically relevant to the job at hand.

3. Don't waste your own time. A hiring manager spends ten seconds on a resume to decide if she'll reject it or not. These ten seconds include your cover letter. Don't let your cover letter waste your ten-second opportunity. The rule of a resume is that every single line of the resume sells you. This is true of the cover letter, too. In fact, it's shorter, so it should sell with more punch. Every sentence of the cover letter should give a specific reason for hiring you, because you never know which sentence will catch the reader's eye during your precious ten seconds.

4. Format strategically. Bullets work well in a cover letter to highlight your relevant achievements immediately. Odd numbers of bullets are proven to be easier to read than even numbers, so use either three or five. Seven is too many—the list will look so long that people will skip it.

5. Tell the reader the next step. A cover letter introduces a resume, and the point of the resume is to get an interview. So in the cover letter say flat out that you want a phone call or an e-mail, because that's how someone sets up an interview. This call to action makes a nice last paragraph.

6. Say it, and then say it again. Put your e-mail address and phone number at the top of the letter, and on the bottom, too. The hiring manager should not have to hunt for your contact information, because each second of that hunt is a second during which the person could change her mind about calling.

7. Come back to it. If you have the wrong company name in your opening sentence, a spell-checker won't catch it and probably neither will you because it's very hard to catch errors when you've been rewriting the same letter for an hour. So come back to the letter in two hours, proofread it, and then send. You'll be amazed at the errors you catch and grateful that you caught them.

8. Follow up. You have to. I know it's a discouraging call to make because odds are that you won't get through to a real person. And if you do get through to a real person, he will likely give you no information. But there is a very slim chance that you will get someone on the phone who will take a good look at your resume just because you called, and that will get you the interview. That's why you need to make the call—because it just might work. Besides, picking up the phone is a lot easier than finding another job opening and writing another cover letter.

These eight steps might seem a lot at first, but once you get some practice, it'll feel natural to approach a cover letter like a piece of direct mail. And like all rules, you will be grateful for guidelines because they mean you don't have to reinvent the wheel every time to be effective.

CHAPTER THREE

Hunting for a Job Is Not a Task, It's a Lifestyle

The majority of job hunters are younger than thirty-five. In fact, among eighteen- to twenty-four-year-olds, 60 percent are looking for work. One poll showed that a third of people in their twenties are scanning want ads and registering with headhunting firms on the first day of their new jobs. This means that the job hunt has changed from being an event to being a constant.

But the hunt is not for more money. It's for more interesting work and a better personal life. So what can you do to make sure you get a job that will encourage new experiences both at work and at home?

Ask a lot of questions in the interview. Older people might tell younger people that there are many questions that are off-limits in an interview. For example, "Can I leave every Wednesday at five to go bike riding with my friends?" But this sort of question is quite common from younger workers.

Trust yourself when it comes to asking questions. According to David Morrison, founder and president of the market research firm Twentysomething, Inc., "Workers who gather information via networking, information on the Internet, and word of mouth ask much better questions in interviews."

Concentrate your energy on finding the right manager as opposed to the right position. There is no reason to be limited by the job description—you can always pick up extra work that increases your experience and exposure.

But a checked-out manager can limit you. So seek managers who will look out for you in the company and make sure you get on good projects. Also, look for a manager who will shepherd you through challenging projects so that you develop new skills.

Look for a benevolent form of micromanagement. A company that is concerned with retaining young people and has hired consultants to help them will be well aware of hands-on management. So ask potential employers about their management training programs. And don't rely completely on what your prospective manager says. Listen to how he or she says it.

"People have a tendency to manage based on their personality type," said Rob Toomey, a trainer at Speed-Reading People. People's speech patterns reveal their management styles.

"Someone who progresses through a conversation step-by-step, methodically, giving details" will manage you carefully and with great interest. The converse is someone who talks in "long paragraphs with semicolons and dashes, with topics that change mid-sentence. This person will be a big-picture thinker and most likely will not manage you closely."

Learn tricks to find this sort of manager faster. Once you know what you're looking for, you need tools for making the job hunt process tolerable. Looking for a job is draining. You need to develop skills that allow you to be great at your current job while you look for the next job. This chapter will give you tips on managing your life and your hunt so that both can flourish simultaneously. Budgeting, for example, will give you more time, and cold-calling will give you faster results. And an optimistic attitude will take you farther than anything else.

8. BUDGET FOR A LONG JOB HUNT AND HOPE FOR A SHORT ONE

When you lose your job, or even if you're worried about it, the most important thing you can do for your career is aggressively save your money. The average job hunt takes at least four months. If your salary is above average, then so is the estimated length of your job hunt. Money in the bank will afford you the time you need to hunt. The more time you have to hunt, the less likely you are to have to settle for a job you don't like.

Even in the face of this knowledge, many people start their job hunt with a level of optimism (or denial) that allows them to continue their I-have-a-job spending patterns. Losing a job is like death—even if you saw it coming, you are sad. Most people cope with sadness by spending money: on clothes, on dinners, on baseball tickets, and on all-day spa deals. You can increase the odds of getting a job you love if you start a job hunt with an honest assessment of how much money you will need to live on for the duration of your job hunt.

Maybe you are one of those really optimistic people. Optimism is good. But optimism with money in the bank is better. For you, it might take a few months of job hunting for you to cut your spending. You might send out resumes for jobs that are better than the job you just lost.

If you don't get a job in a couple of months, you need to admit that you are just like everyone else and your hunt will take half a year. At this point, you probably have had no interviews, or if you have had interviews, the hiring manager has said casually, "We culled your resume from a pile of three hundred qualified applicants."

But there's still time to adjust your budget so you can last longer. Cut your budget as much as you can without losing your housing, your friends, or your sanity. If it's too late and you don't have enough money to last six months, then cut your job expectations, too, so that you can land a job more quickly. Having a little money to spare allows you to be a little bit picky about the job you take. When you're broke you have to take the first job that comes along.

Still not scared enough to save? If you don't cut back at this point, you'll want to cut back later, but it'll be too late. Early on you can cut back on things that don't matter that much, like movies, facials, and extra toppings on your pizza. Later, you may have to also cut back on things that matter a lot, like your cell phone (even though you put that number on resumes you sent out) and your health insurance (you figure, you're healthy, so you can stop paying insanely high COBRA fees).

Then you realize you have erred. You hear about someone in your position who got sick and had to go to a scary hospital because they were uninsured and they got even sicker while they were there. So you take a job at Starbucks, or the Starbucks equivalent in your neighborhood—one of those big retail chains that offer bad jobs and good health insurance. You find yourself living off your Starbucks salary, miserable, and drowning your sorrows in free lattes.

This scenario is grim, so think about it at the beginning of your hunt, when you are figuring out how long your money has to last. That way you are less likely to end up in job hunt hell. A key to a successful job hunt is giving yourself enough time to succeed, and in this case, time is money.

9. MAKE A STRATEGIC MOVE TO YOUR MOM'S HOUSE

In the list of what's hot and what's not, blowing all your money on an overpriced apartment is out and sleeping on the twin bed at your parents' house is in. Bobby Jackson is a senior at Williams College. When he graduates, he will move back to Washington, D.C., and look for a public relations job from the comfort of his parents' home. Jackson typifies the remarkable shift of intergenerational attitudes when he declares, "I love hanging out with my parents."

According to the market research company Twentysomething Inc., 65 percent of college seniors expect to live with their parents after graduation. The job Web site MonsterTRAK reports that 50 percent of the class of 2003 was still living at home in 2006. "Boomerangers" is what analysts call the twentysomethings who move back home, and the consensus among researchers (who grew up in an era when moving back was a sign of failure) is that being a boomeranger is a strategically sound way to head toward an independent life.

Neil Howe, coauthor of *Millennials Rising: The Next Great Generation,* says that moving back with parents is a way to avoid wasting a lot of time. According to Howe, when it comes to careers, "Boomerangers want to get it right the first time." If you don't have to worry about paying rent, you have more flexibility to wait for the right job and to take a job that feels very right but pays very poorly. The rise of the prestigious but unpaid internship intersects perfectly with the rise of the boomeranger.

Today it's almost impossible to become self-sufficient on an entry-level salary, especially in coastal cities, where rents are skyrocketing. Barbara Mitchell, professor of sociology at Simon Fraser University and author of *The Boomerang Age: Transition to Adulthood in Families*, says, "Most entry-level jobs won't be permanent or stable," so saving money is difficult. Twentysomethings have to manage the costs of rent, college loans, and insurance premiums, all of which are rising faster than wages.

With these economic factors, it's hard for a boomeranger to leave again, and according to Mitchell, many underestimate the amount of time they'll be staying. Bobby Jackson, for example, figures that, "Most entry-level jobs pay thirty thousand dollars. So I'll stay at home for six months and save ten to fifteen thousand." This plan would work only if he didn't buy work clothes, go out with friends, or pay taxes—at least not with his own money.

And this is where the problems start. Boomerangers who think their time with Mom and Dad will last fewer than seven months are statistically delusional and setting themselves up for emotional crisis. The typical stay is so long that researchers don't even count someone as a boomeranger until they've been back home for four months.

Elina Furman knows this problem firsthand: she ended up living with her family until she was twenty-nine, and she does not describe the time as a constant joyride. In fact, she says, after the initial thrill of college graduation and the return of home-cooked meals, boomerangers find themselves in the midst of crisis—usually financial or relationship-oriented—and suffering from feelings of isolation and loss of self-esteem.

As a veteran of boomerang life, Furman supplies methods for success in her book, *Boomerang Nation: How to Survive Living with Your Parents...the Second Time Around.* She recommends making changes to your bedroom so it reflects who you are now. Otherwise, it becomes a "permanent purgatory" of high school trophies and reminders that you are not where you want to be. Also, she says, "Do your own laundry and cook for yourself" because it's more empowering than reverting to living like a seventeen-year-old. Her chapters on financial planning and exit strategies describe other dangerous pitfalls of boomerang life.

And Furman warns, "The stigma is more than people realize." (Which explains why the only people who were willing to let me interview them on this subject were those who were just starting or those who had made it out of the house again.) Older generations are often stuck in outdated attitudes about the transition to adulthood, and they ask grating questions like, "You live where? At your age? What's wrong with you?"

But in fact, moving back home is probably the first step in the post-boomer revolution of the workplace. Expectations for work are higher than ever—it should be fulfilling, fun, and accommodating of a substantial personal life. The logical way to meet such revolutionary expectations is to start out on a revolutionary path. So hold your head high as a boomeranger, but don't leave your dirty dishes in the sink.

10. COLD-CALLING WILL EMPOWER YOU

Cold-calling is for champions. It used to be that cold-calling was for the losers so low on the corporate ladder, they were falling off the last rung. But today it's clear that cold-calling is an art form, and people who are good at it can do a lot for themselves—most notably get a job.

Skeptical? Well, I'm not sure you have much of a choice. Fewer than half of all available jobs are advertised and most people don't get jobs through listings. So how are you going to find them? Your best odds are networking. But most people exhaust their network in a month, and most job hunts last for at least four months. So after networking, the best thing to do is probably cold-calling.

Everyone knows that it's really hard to make a cold call, so people will respect you for trying. But you'll get self-respect, too, because if you only respond to ads, then you are basically running a passive job hunt, waiting for something to pop up on your computer screen. If you approach companies you're interested in, whether or not they post jobs, then you are taking control of your hunt and actively trying to attain your goals.

Think of all the times in life you regret. Usually it was when you didn't take a more active role in your life; when you didn't take control of your life. In this sense, you can't lose making a cold call. No one ever says to themselves, "I wish I hadn't been so aggressive in trying to get what I wanted." If you are aggressive and you don't get what you want, you probably weren't going to get it anyway. So might as well go down swinging.

The easiest and most obvious cold call is not really even cold. It's a follow-up call. This is what you do when you've been sending tons of resumes out and you are receiving no interviews: after you send your resume, call the hiring manager to say you really want the job.

You will probably have to dig a lot to find the hiring manager. But hey, you have all day to dig, right? You'll have to call human resources. Maybe some random dialing within the department. Maybe some Googling. But you can find someone who sounds like he might be the hiring person and ask who the hiring person is. Sooner or later someone will tell you.

Once you get that person, pitch yourself on the phone. That pitch has to be good. Friendly, informative, fast. This is the crux of the art form. Then, ask if you can come in for an interview. Even though the advertisement says no calls, a call is a great way to get someone to pay attention to you when there's a huge pile of resumes.

You can use this same tactic even if there is no job offered and you have not sent a resume. Just call someone in a department that interests you—business development in an advertising agency; marketing at a Fortune 500 company. Tell the person that you're interested in that industry, you really admire the company, and you'd like to schedule an informational interview. If you ask for a job the person can say no, outright. But information? That's not so easy a no. Of course, the person has information. And you'd be surprised at how many people are willing to give it if you just ask.

Then you need to be charming. And smart. If the person loves you, she might make a spot for you in her department. Or maybe she has a friend who is hiring. Who knows? You never will until you try.

It's all about odds. You need to have the ego strength to dial these people all day. You only need one person to say yes. That yes means you expanded your network that day. And all those people who say no, you'll never see them again. They are gone. No need to feel bad or embarrassed. It's over. Move on.

The odds are not great that the cold call will work every time, but you only need it to work really well once and then you're done. You have a job.

CHAPTER FOUR

An Interview Is a Test You Can Study For

Hiring managers don't hire the most qualified person. They hire the person they want to work with the most. Whether this is fair is not up for discussion because the philosophical and de facto practices of corporate hiring aren't going to change any time soon. However, we can discuss how to get hired when being qualified is a small factor in the decision.

Too many people have had slews of interviews with no offers. To be sure, you need to work at getting interviews, but you also need to work hard at turning an interview into a job. Here are six steps between landing and going to the interview that will help you get an offer.

1. Research the company. Comb through every section of the company's Web site and memorize it as if you were cramming for a test. Unlike a test, though, you won't have a chance to spout the six facts you learned about the company during the interview.

Rather, there will be a random, fleeting moment when a relevant fact you gained from the site will be the perfect response to something the interviewer says. To find the right comment for that fleeting moment, you'll need wide knowledge and good judgment. The overall goal is to seem as though you monitor the company independently of your desperate need for a job.

2. Get the right outfit. Corporate America has a uniform; wear it. People like to hire people who look like them, and clothing is the easiest way to make this impression. An interview is not the time to dress to express your true self. In fact, no one needs to know your true self at the office. You will fit in and work best with others by keeping eccentricities to a minimum. Each company has a variation on "the uniform," so loiter near the office ahead of time and spy on its workers to get a sense of the corporate dress code.

3. Prepare stock answers. Most interview questions are standard and, surprisingly enough, have standard answers. Take the question, "Why do you want to leave your current job?" The correct answer incorporates phrases like, "I am looking for a company like this one," and "Your company offers a unique opportunity that is a perfect fit for me." Learn these answers before the interview and be prepared to deliver them with a special flair so they don't seem rehearsed. There are three or four good books that list interview questions and how you should answer them. The one I have used successfully is *The Complete Q&A Job Interview Book,* by Jeffrey B. Allen.

4. Go to the gym. Taking charge of the first fifteen seconds of an interview is critical. An interviewer will judge you first and most significantly on nonverbal cues, and having a great interview outfit alone may not be enough to make the best impression. This is because thin, good-looking people are more likely to get hired than overweight, less attractive people. If you have scheduled the interview already, it's probably too late to drop forty pounds, but go to the gym anyway. By using your chest and back muscles to lift weights, you'll stand up straighter in the interview—which shows poise and self-confidence. Also take a run on the treadmill. The more energy you expend now, the more relaxed you'll be at the interview, and being calm will help you seem more confident.

5. Prepare to close the deal. Leave nothing open-ended when you walk out of the interview. This means saying at the end, "I would really like this job. Do you have any reservations about hiring me?" This is scary to say because the interviewer might have reservations you can't overcome. But closers get the contracts, and you need to be a closer in interviews. Risk hearing any reservations because it's better to confront them and fail than to never try. You have nothing to lose.

When I tried this, the hiring manager told me her reservations (which were large). After I countered them one by one, she was so impressed that she offered me a job on the spot. But I had also done my homework. I had memorized the company information and the answers to the 100 most common interview questions, plus I managed my impression during those first fifteen seconds as if my life depended on it.

6. *Practice, practice, practice.* Maybe your friends will be helpful in a mock interview situation. Even if your friend does a terrible job pretending to be an interviewer, you get practice interviewing with someone who doesn't know how to do the job. You can bet, though, that someone in the career counseling office of your college knows what she is doing in this regard. Career centers are evaluated based on the career success of their graduates, so most centers are happy to field your phone calls, no matter how long ago you graduated. Ask someone there to do a mock interview with you. The feedback you get will probably be very useful.

11. THERE *ARE* STUPID QUESTIONS, SO DON'T ASK THEM

Most interviews pause when the hiring manager says, "Do you have any questions for me?" In a world of workplace transparency, the most common response to this question would be, "No. I have no questions. I am sick of job hunting. Give me a job."

But alas, you must play the interview game. So ask three or four questions as a way to convey that you have options, even if you don't. Your questions should convey: "I'm trying to find out more about this position to decide if I'm interested."

But you cannot say that flat out without sounding like an arrogant pain in the butt. You have to imply this message. Like the rest of the interview, what you imply, purposely or inadvertently, is as important as what you say. So craft your questions carefully before you get to the interview, and have some extras in case a few turn out to be inappropriate.

Here are some types of questions to avoid:

"How many hours a day do you work?" This is a quality-of-life question. Quality of life is important, and if you need to leave at 5 p.m. every day, that's fair. But while most people will tell you they respect that request, few jobs actually will, in fact, be able to accommodate that. So instead of talking about reasonable hours, observe the office to see the hours people keep.

People who have no respect for reasonable hours will make that clear in an interview, either by announcing it, or by doing something like scheduling the interview for the middle of the day on Saturday. If you have to make a point of asking about reasonable hours in the interview, then you're probably in trouble. If the office culture is long hours, then even if the interviewer tells you that you can go home at 6 p.m., you will be marginalized among workaholics. So don't ask directly.

If you get through a full interview and the hiring manager never reveals that she has a life outside of work, there's no need to ask: she doesn't. If you are unsure about the situation, conduct some independent research. Park your car in the company lot and stalk unsuspecting employees to see when they come and go. Or, go to a pay phone and anonymously call the interviewer at 7 p.m. four nights in a row to see if she's still at the office. Just don't ask about it in the interview.

"If this company were an animal which one would it be?"
Nothing abstract. Please. This nutcase-question throws off an interview and is appropriate to test what someone does under pressure. But, as the interviewee, it is not your job to initiate pressure. (Note, though, that you need to be prepared to field this question about yourself—that is, what animal would you be.)

Most hiring decisions are made based on chemistry. Your number-one goal when you interview for a job is to get the person asking the questions to like you. So you should ask questions that make this person feel comfortable.

If you can do it without sounding like a brownnose, ask the person something about how she got to be so great. For example: "Why did you decide to work for this company?"

This question implies that you're interested in other people and that you respect the interviewer.

"What needs to be accomplished in this position in the next six months?" This is a useless question at the end of an interview, but an essential one for the beginning. So ask this question within the first five minutes of the interview, and then tailor everything you say to address the goals of the position.

The overall rule that should guide your preparation is never stop selling yourself in an interview, even when you pretend to stop selling yourself in order to ask a question.

12. TELL A FEW STORIES

When someone asks, "What do you do?" a one-word answer will put your career on ice. You need to have a creative and interesting answer. When you want to establish a connection with someone, a good story rather than a rote, typical response provides social glue. When you want to impress someone, a story is more memorable than a list of achievements.

Early in my career, I interviewed for a job as a user interface (UI) designer. I analyzed the best places to put buttons and links on a given screen so that they were easiest to use. The hiring manager asked me how I got involved in UI design.

I could have said, "I thought it looked interesting so I gave it a try and I was good at it." But anyone can answer the very standard how-did-you-find-your-career question with that answer.

So instead, I told this story: My ex-boyfriend was a programmer, and he worked from home while I was in school. He plastered UI designs all over our bedroom wall and our living room floor so that he could think them through. Finally, I told him that if he was going to mess up the apartment, then he had to be the one to clean it, and I handed him the toilet scrubber. We argued about who had extra time for cleaning and who didn't and finally he said, "Fine. I'll clean, but you do the UI design." And to his surprise, I did.

The interviewer liked that story and I got the job. In fact, every time I have been able to tell good stories in interviews, I have gotten the job.

When it comes to your career, have a one-minute story ready. It's the story of you—how you got to where you are and what your achievements are. When someone asks a question like, "How did you get into advertising?" tell your story.

When you interview, tell stories. You know you're going to encounter the question, "What are your strengths?" Don't give a list. It's not persuasive. Tell a story about how you did something amazing by using your strengths. This way you tell the hiring manager something memorable and you get in a bit about your achievements.

Once you get the job, keep telling stories as a way to promote yourself within the company. No one knows you the first month of your job, so they ask questions like, "Where were you before this?" or "What sort of experience do you have?" These are times to tell your story. If you are funny, make it funny. If you are not funny, let your story show your vulnerability.

Your success at your job will depend on your finding someone to help you navigate the corporate ladder: you need to find a mentor; you need to get on plum projects; you need to show people you are smart and interesting so that they want to help you. Don't assume that your work speaks for itself. It doesn't. Most people will have no idea what you have done or what you do now. You need to tell them. And the best way to tell them without sounding boring or self-obsessed is to tell good stories.

Still feeling queasy about talking yourself up to people? Check out the book *Brag!,* by Peggy Klaus, the master of self-promotion. Worried that you don't know how to tell a story? Give business books a break and take a look at *Flash*

Fiction, edited by James Thomas. This is an anthology of two-page stories that have similar pacing as those you'll want to tell at the office.

Spinning a good story is difficult. But building a career without a story is even more difficult. So you'd better start spinning.

13. SALARY NEGOTIATION IS WHEN YOU CAN EARN $1,000 IN A MINUTE

Don't be afraid to negotiate your salary. Once you get an offer, you know you're the top candidate. So have some confidence. Recognize that the people who have the most successful careers are those who are not afraid of negotiating. The best way to get into that category is to force yourself to ask for more money, even if it's difficult.

In fact, even if you don't get more money, you will feel good about having asked for it. There is a lot to be said for being a person who always asks. Not asking is a bad habit. If you shut yourself down in this instance, you're probably doing it in other places in your life, too. But if you take a chance to ask for more here, you will be more comfortable doing it again once you get the job.

Here's a four-step process for doing well in salary negotiations.

1. Don't disclose your pay requirements during the interview process. The first person to provide numbers establishes the range. If you give a number first, the interviewer will either tell you you're in the same ballpark as him or you're too high.

If you ask for less than the interviewer is considering, you'll probably get it—and never find out that you could have earned more. So interviewers always want you to disclose your requirements first. (Do not try to remedy this situation by giving an unreasonably high number, because then you will sound unreasonable.)

Your first line of defense is to say you'd like to talk about salary once you have an offer. Still, a good interviewer will persevere. To successfully avoid saying a number, you need to be ready with other things to say. A good start is to say you'd like to know the range the position pays. Whatever number the interviewer gives, you can say, "That will be a fine starting point." (You will ask for more later.) If he keeps pressing you, tell him you think your salary history is not relevant because this is a different job.

In the end, you might have to say flat out that you're not going to give a number. Someone who has pressed you very hard for a number will respect this answer—after all, no one presses this hard unless he understands that having this number gives the hiring side a huge advantage.

2. Get the whole offer in writing before you ask for more. Here's why (and you should remember this for when the tables are turned): Let's say the job pays a salary and a performance bonus, but you don't know about the bonus part. If you do not get a written offer specifying the pay elements before you start negotiating, then you might negotiate a higher base salary but lose a portion of your bonus. That's because the bonus gives your hiring manager some "wiggle room." She can take it off the table before you know you're supposed to receive it. (Then she can report back to her boss and say, "I saved us $5,000.") Get the full offer in writing so you know what you have to work with during your bargaining.

Once you have that written offer, ask for a night to think about it and come back with a counteroffer. Admittedly, you may hate confrontation and feel you're a poor negotiator, but you have nothing to lose and you're likely to get more money. Plus you will get better at this each time you do it. Remember, almost no one loses a written offer because of asking for more money.

3. Go home and form a plan. To know what to ask for in negotiations, you *must* know the pay range for your position. Check out salary surveys online and in trade journals. Do not quote any numbers from surveys conducted more than two years ago. Get more recent information. Talk with friends in similar jobs or recruiters who regularly fill this type of position in your geographic region. Find the top of the salary range and ask for that. Show the hiring manager your research and remind her why you are worth the top of the range.

If you are fortunate enough to find out that your offer is already in the high end of your salary range, then propose taking on more responsibilities so you can ask for slightly more pay. Suppose you are a marketing manager with a background in technical writing. You can say that while most marketing managers pass off technical writing in marketing documents to someone else, you will handle this yourself. This entitles you to ask for slightly more.

4. Know yourself. Each person is compensated in different ways—and not always monetarily. For instance, if you love what you do, you may not mind earning less than your neighbor who has the same degree. Likewise if you have a shorter commute.

Friends can advise you, but you are the one in the job, and you must decide if you want it, regardless of the size of your paycheck. No salary survey can tell you that. Decide what's important to you and what trade-offs you're willing to make pay-wise, but be honest with yourself. Don't give up being paid more because you hate negotiating. Self-knowledge and good negotiation skills—plus a little chutzpah—will help ensure that you earn what you deserve starting with your next job.

CHAPTER FIVE

Corporate Life Is Too Risky—Start Your Own Business

Feeling stuck? Uninspired? Do your workdays have a chronic copy-machine glow? Then get out. Start your own business and then you can hire someone else to make copies. Or, better yet, use your entrepreneurial strength to banish the copy-slave position from the workplace.

Entrepreneurship used to be an inclination that festered until a midlife crisis. But the entrepreneurship bug isn't something that hits only in middle age. Today, most new businesses are started by people under thirty-four—if they're doing it, why can't you? Don't be stifled by your age or lack of experience. And don't be scared off by the stock reasons people spew to dissuade you when you mention entrepreneurship. If you develop the key qualities of a good entrepreneur, you have a good shot at launching a successful business.

It's true that you might not make enough money at first, but who is making enough money at the beginning of their career anyway? The few who pull down six figures probably spent six figures on grad school and are paying it back, with interest. If you never switch careers, never risk being a beginner, never bet on yourself, you will put your career in a coma.

Some may argue that you can be entrepreneurial in a large company. But large companies suck up fast-paced, fun, innovative small businesses and make them boring, and then they tell you, in an interview, that the position you are considering is very entrepreneurial. It's not. If it were entrepreneurial it would be too big a wild card to fit into a corporate hierarchy.

At this point in loyalty-free corporate life, it may be a higher risk to work for someone else. Seventy-six percent of new businesses last for at least two years. Sure, most do not last as long as, say, General Motors. But are you looking to run a multinational company, or are you looking to get control over your time and your workload so you can have fun and preserve your personal life?

Don't listen to those people who tell you small businesses are risky. Listen to Matt Rivers, owner of Pump House Surf Shop, who went into business when he was seventeen. He worked at restaurants to earn spending money but saved most of it. And when his favorite surf shop went out of business, he decided to buy it. Matt didn't know much about running a business, but he knew a lot about surfing. Friends and family work in the store, and wholesalers mentored him as he went along. And the store is open only in the summer, which allowed him to finish school. To Matt, the biggest risk was that he'd have to grow up and get a job that wouldn't allow him to surf.

Figure out what you want your daily life to look like, and then decide which route is most likely to get you to that—working for someone else or starting your own business. This chapter will help you see possibilities. You will see how corporate structures undervalue the contribution that young people make from within the company—and what people have done to get around this problem. Also, you'll find tools to evaluate whether you have the character traits and the ideas to make it on your own.

14. CORPORATE AMERICA UNDERVALUES PEOPLE IN THEIR TWENTIES

At top-tier universities like Harvard and Carnegie Mellon, 30 to 40 percent of graduates end up starting their own business after five years, and the trend is poised to go up. Business schools are falling over each other to show that they are good training ground for entrepreneurship. "For the most ambitious young people, the corporate ladder is obsolete," declares Paul Graham, partner at Y Combinator, a Cambridge, MA–based venture capital firm that funds startups almost exclusively from very young people.

This trend is fueled in large part because the entry-level job inherently undervalues someone who is bright and driven. Paul Graham sees entrepreneurship as the great escape. According to Graham, for the last hundred years everyone started out at the bottom. Even if the candidate held extreme promise, corporations made him a trainee on the bottom rung so he didn't get a big head. Graham writes, "The most productive young people will *always* be undervalued by large organizations, because the young have no performance to measure yet, and any error in guessing their ability will tend toward the mean."

So, if you are smart and energetic, you might be better off working for yourself. Alexis Ohanian and Steve Huffman started their own company before they even graduated from the University of Virginia. After graduation they ran their company, Reddit, out of their Cambridge apartment.

Huffman turned down a job offer at a software company in Virginia so that he could write his own software for Reddit.

The value of people in their twenties is touted fervently at Google, a company always on the lookout to buy companies from young entrepreneurs. On a blog entry about a conference for entrepreneurs in their early twenties, Chris Sacca, principal for new business development at Google, wrote, "I was instantly struck by the sheer energy of the crowd. No one was running off to check in with their assistant or jump onto a mindless conference call with sales finance."

Graham estimates that a top programmer can work for $80,000 a year in a large company, but he can be thirty-six times more productive without corporate trappings (e.g., a boss, killed projects, interruptions) and will generate something worth $3 million in that same year if he is working on his own. Before you balk at those figures, consider that Ohanian and Huffman started their company in June 2005 and by November 2005 they received a buyout offer (which they declined in favor of continuing to build the company on their own).

But not everyone is sitting on a great idea. Here are some things you can do in the meantime. For those of you who eventually want to start your own business—once you find an idea—use the time beforehand to learn the right skills. Jennifer Floren, CEO of Experience and an entrepreneur herself, recommends going to a small company "where you will usually be able to see firsthand what each part of the company does. At a big company you won't get such wide exposure." Also, she says, "Look for opportunities to be creative or take a leadership role, two good types of experience for an entrepreneur to have."

While you're doing this, keep thinking of ideas. Huffman thought of ideas all the time—in the shower, in class, lying in bed. Make time for ideas to come to you. But you might be like Ohanian, who did not think of tons of ideas but helped Huffman make use of his ideas. Huffman came very close to taking that job in Virginia. Ohanian had to work hard to convince his friend to start Reddit. Ohanian saw the brilliance and potential of the idea, even though it wasn't his own.

Maybe you're someone who thinks of ideas, maybe you're someone who recognizes a good one. Maybe you can do both. Just make sure you are able to get the full value of your energy and intelligence. There is no reason you need to be doing mindless work as "training" for corporate life. And there's no reason you can't start your own company and sell it to the corporations that misjudged you because of your age.

15. CHECKLIST FOR STARTING YOUR OWN BUSINESS

People used to think that entrepreneurs are born, but current research reveals that the traits entrepreneurs need can be taught, and that you can prime yourself for success by focusing on finding the right idea for you and your network of contacts. Andrew Zacharakis, professor of entrepreneurship at Babson College, says research points to three important traits of an entrepreneur:

1. Have knowledge of your market. Just because you know biotech is hot doesn't mean you should start a company in the sector. You need a concept that is valid and marketable, and you're not going to come up with one unless you really know your market. Matt Rivers bought out a failed surf shop because he knew he could run it better; after all, he was one of its regular customers. He also understood how to advertise to his market: he rides on the top surf team on the East Coast, and his shop sponsors the team—thus targeting his demographic to a pinpoint.

2. Build an extensive network. Matt knows all the top surfers on the East Coast, but they were not the guys sewing the wet suits. So he quickly developed rapport with surf suppliers, because at the beginning he had very little cash. He'd sell a shirt to a customer and with that money he'd buy two more shirts from wholesalers. At that pace, he needed vendors who liked him because they weren't making any money off his phone calls.

You need a network to start and grow a business, and networks do not come to people who are not likeable. For those of you who are scheming to be someone you're not, forget it. You don't get likeable by being fake. A great primer on networking is *Never Eat Alone: And Other Secrets to Success, One Relationship at a Time,* by Keith Ferrazzi. When he talks about networking, he talks about being liked. He says, "If people like you, they will help you, so instead of concentrating on getting favors, focus on being likeable."

3. Be committed to the business. You are going to have a lot of nights eating Ramen noodles. If all you want to do is surf, low income is fine: waves are free. But many people will need to carefully set up a life that can withstand a very low budget. Rich Farrell, founder of the technology company FullArmor, feels lucky he started when he was right out of college and his parents' basement seemed like reasonable living quarters. "I couldn't do that now," he says. "My wife wouldn't live in the basement and my parents wouldn't live with my two-year-old."

But when it comes to entrepreneurial chops, commitment isn't just about suffering, it's about passion. You have to love what you do because you'll be doing it 24/7 for a while. Whether you're in the office or at home, you'll be thinking about it all the time—you won't be able to stop. You also need to love it because loving what you do is a key factor in success. A study of Harvard Business School grads showed that people who went into a profession they loved ended up making more money than people who went into a profession for money.

A successful entrepreneur also needs the manic energy that comes from passion and commitment. When you own the company, you set the pace and the standards. Remember the day at the office last month when you were upset and tired from worrying about your personal life the night before, so you surfed the Internet all day? You can't do that when you own the company. Most small business owners start out working eighty-hour weeks and wishing they needed less sleep.

Let's say you have those three requirements. It's not enough. You need one more.

4. Be ready to fail fast and move on. Most business leaders fail once or twice before hitting it big. Think of failure as a necessary career step and don't trip; recognize when things are going poorly, fail fast, learn, and get another idea.

Y Combinator is a venture capital firm that holds a contest for early-stage start-ups every summer. Phil Yuen won one of its competitions and he left his job at Microsoft to build software that could find errors on people's Web sites. But by the end of the summer, the company hadn't taken off. Instead of worrying about his lack of success, Phil came back to Y Combinator in the fall with another business idea of designing software that would allow people to pay each other via their cell phones. He got his funding and founded TextPayMe. Phil was not scared of failure because he had a good supply of ideas for companies.

Another way to ensure smooth failure is to protect your basic necessities. Think of starting a business as gambling: when you go to Vegas, never bet your plane fare home. When you start a business, don't bet everything you have, unless your parents will show up at your front door to bail you out.

Some of you will be like Matt, looking for a lifestyle over everything else, and some of you will be like Phil, dying to create something out of nothing. Some of you will be both. But do a solid self-assessment. You don't need to be born with the traits of a good entrepreneur, but you should cultivate them before you take the leap.

16. MONEY IS GROWING ON TREES, ALMOST

It might shock you to hear that it's easier to find money to fund your business idea than it is to find an idea. A good idea, that is. There are many kinds of good ideas. For example, a small business that will not grow but will sustain the lifestyle you want for yourself: opening a gift shop on a Hawaiian beach. Or one that will be big. Big in that you can grow it to become a big player or you can sell it to a big player.

Your goal should be to raise only the amount of money you absolutely need, because you will either be paying interest or you will be giving the money source a percentage of your company. The two most common financing techniques used by startups with less than five employees are loans from relatives and borrowing against credit cards.

The fastest source for money when you have no money is, of course, your credit card. If you can get one of those zero-percent interest offers, the credit card option starts looking particularly good.

But, "if you're not prepared to lose your own money, you should look for money from other sources," advises Ed Arvidson, a business plan consultant at Belissimo. "Don't spend your own money if the loss will devastate you."

"Angel" investors are constantly looking to put money into companies that will grow big. If you have this kind of idea, there are plenty of angels to choose from. A good place to start is online, looking for people who invest in early-stage companies in your market.

The important issue will be finding someone smart and experienced who can help you grow the company to the next stage. In exchange for giving up a percentage of the ownership of your company, you should get solid mentoring as well as money. The network and advice that an angel offers is what separates the amazing ones from the mediocre.

If your business will not be big, then your pool of angels is pretty much limited to people who know you well and want to do you a favor. But there are ways you can structure a deal so that your friends and family feel like it's a decent investment. Arvidson suggests paying higher interest rates than a bank. You could also offer a piece of the business. For example, agree to pay back the loan plus pay 5 percent of the business profits. Arvidson says the latter deal should be one of last resort. The 5 percent is a limitless amount over which you have little control, and the angel is likely to be interested in monthly financial statements and other paperwork that will be burdensome to you.

When putting together your pitch, it's important to be up front about the risks involved and the expected rate of return. Your presentation should be thorough and professional, even if you know the prospective angel well. But on some level, these people come to the table based on their trust and respect for you. And this trust and respect is what you are trading on when it comes to angels.

"Start by listing everyone you can think of who trusts you," recommends Tom Matzen, a coach for entrepreneurs. For most people this is a list of about fifty people. Put everyone on the list, even if they don't have money and even if you can't find them; people who trust you might refer you to someone else, and just seeing the name on the list might remind you of someone else you know who does have money to invest.

Then divide the list into As, Bs, and Cs. The As are people who have a lot of money and a lot of investments. The Bs are financially stable people who would think very, very hard before forking over $25,000. The Cs are people who don't really have the financial resources to invest in your operation, but they might vouch for you to someone they know who does have money.

Practice your pitch on the C group. Send an e-mail to the list briefly outlining the proposition. If someone responds, then go ahead and meet with that person to practice your dog and pony show. Remember to personally guarantee that the investors will get their money back—you might not be sure when, but they will get it back. Then go to your B list and do the same thing. By the time you get to your A list, you'll be ready with your pitch—in fact, you'll be good at it, and you'll be much more likely to land investors.

The most important thing, no matter what kind of business you are pitching, is to not give up early. If there are no investors, you might have a clunker of an idea on your hands. But a little rejection happens to a lot of good ideas. So brace yourself as you look for funding and keep going right past the rejections.

CHAPTER SIX

First-Time Managers Do Not Need to Suck

The first time I got a big management position I tried to overhaul all of corporate America from my new-manager cubicle. I surreptitiously implemented affirmative action, and though I hate to admit this, I hired people who were not totally qualified. I gave people with scattered track records the chances of their lifetimes, and when they failed I compensated for them. I mentored people at all hours of the day and my work suffered. I snuffed out sexual harassment at a speed that only someone looking too hard for it could manage. Finally, I got a reputation for caring more about making people's lives better than making my boss's life better. It was a deserved reputation, and I was fired.

It hurts me even now to say it was a deserved firing. But it taught me a good lesson: the company comes first. And my job was to please my boss. Which is everyone's job. You get an opportunity to manage people because you are going to make things better for the company. The company wants happy workers, but not at the expense of effective workers.

As a manager you are in a position to make people's lives better. You can give them more interesting work, better coaching, more flexibility—all the things you have always wanted in a job, you can give to other people. You should do that.

Here's another piece of advice for new managers: success is about balance. A good manager balances the needs of her company and the needs of her employees. After that, a good manager uses her power over people's lives to make the world a better place.

The cynics of the world will say, "That's not realistic. I never got that." But don't ask yourself if you ever got that. Ask yourself if you ever gave it. It is possible to go through your life doing good deeds and just trusting that they'll come back to you in some way. Management is the power to make a difference. You need to do that without wondering what you'll get in return.

That said, you could do more great things if you managed really well and got more power. Don't forget that.

If you have never managed people before, you're lucky to be reading this chapter first. Those of you who have already done some management understand that it's difficult to be good. This chapter will help you make yourself great.

17. DO YOUR OWN WORK LAST

First-time managers are generally nightmares to work for. This is true for people who start their own business and have to manage a growing staff, and it is a problem for people who do an entry-level job well and get promoted.

The problem is that being good at getting things done has very little to do with being good at helping other people get things done. The expression "If you can't play then coach" is relevant here. Coaching and playing are two different skills. Being a good player does not mean you'll be a good coach.

So take your transition to manager very seriously since you have no idea how much talent you have. Work hard to avoid typical pitfalls of new managers. Here are four of the mistakes that undermine a new manager the fastest:

1. *Focusing on tasks instead of people.* Before you were a manager, your number-one job was to accomplish tasks. You were someone with the skills to get something done. Maybe media buying, or programming, or selling. Now your number-one job is to help other people accomplish the tasks in an outstanding way.

Sure, you'll have tasks, too. As a manager you'll have weekly reports, budgets, planning. But your tasks are secondary to helping other people do their tasks. Your job as manager is to get the best work from the people you manage. The measure of how well you're doing as a manager is how well each individual on your team performs.

Ideally, you should be able to show the people you manage how to see themselves differently so that they are able to produce at a higher level than they ever imagined. For one person, this will mean you need to teach organization skills. For another person, you will help her discover what she loves to do and then set her up doing it for you. Each person wants something, and you need to find out what that is. Then help them get it.

In return, your employees will do great work for you. This level of management is superior to task management; helping people perform at their best impacts the quality of your team's work as opposed to just getting the work done.

2. *Being slow to transition.* Moving into any new position requires that you get rid of the stuff from your old position. This means delegating. It means getting over the idea that you were indispensable on any of your old teams. You can't do your new job well if you're still doing your old job.

Delegating your old job should take three days. You find people who are taking a step up when they accept pieces of your old job so that they are excited. You give them an explanation of how to do it and tell them where to go when they have questions.

You're going to tell me that three days are not enough, that you have a very complicated job. But think of it this way: if you died today, your job would be delegated in a couple of days.

Delegating is not enough, though. You have to stop caring. If you are no longer on a project because you got a promotion, then you have to stop obsessing about how the project is doing. Remember how quickly the girl who dumped you hooked up with her next-door neighbor? You need to move that fast, too.

3. Forgetting to manage up. Managing up means steering your team to hit goals that the people above you care about. Figure out what matters to your boss, and your boss's boss, and make that stuff matter to you, too, because you can only impress your boss with your management skill if you are accomplishing things she cares about.

And be loud about your accomplishments. Set measurable goals for yourself and let people above you know that you're meeting them.

Do this right off the bat. People's perceptions of you as a manager will be made during your very first actions. The saying "People judge you in the first two minutes they meet you" is true for management, too. So give people reason right away to think you're doing a good job.

4. Talking more than listening. My sister-in-law Rachel has been a manager for a while. She recently accepted a position in which she is managing three times the number of people she had been managing. Her first step was to go on a sort of listening tour of the organization. She had lunch with people to find out what matters to them. She sat in on groups and even visited some people at home, all in the name of figuring out what matters to them and how she should set up goals for herself.

Consider your own listening tour as soon as you start in a new position. After all, there's no way to figure out what people want without getting them to talk. And the most annoying thing about any manager—new or seasoned—is when he or she just won't shut up.

As with all success, it's about rising above the common denominator. Once you know that most new managers fail, you know to pay close attention to your own transition. When you find yourself at a loss for what to do next, make people your first priority. Be kind and understanding, and demand the best performance they can give. Approach every management problem you have with this thinking and you will be a long way toward defying new-manager odds.

18. IF YOU'RE A MESS AT HOME IT SHOWS AT WORK

Many times, the job of a manager is so multifaceted and detail-laden that the manager loses sight of the big picture. The job of a manager is more than putting your head down and doing the work. It's also looking up to see how everyone else is doing, how they are working together, and how your team fits into the company. In order to be moved into a more strategic role, you need to show that you can manage the team you have and still leave time for big-picture thinking.

Here are five jobs of a manager that are often lost in the muddle of managing smaller, day-to-day issues.

1. Manage conflict. Avoiding conflict is for people who want to lie low and move up by dint of inertia. This plan will take you only so far. At some point you have to meet conflict head-on and show that you can resolve it. Think about this: at the highest levels of management, leaders are essentially gathering competing opinions from the very informed and making a decision based on conflicting recommendations.

Conflict at this level, for example, "Karen is late on every project and I don't want to work with her on the next one," is preparation for larger management challenges. Don't shrink from this stepping-stone by hiding in the sand until the conflict resolves itself. Managing conflict allows you to become an arbitrator and negotiator, and most of all, someone who has developed good judgment on hard calls.

2. Manage your personal life. You are kidding yourself if you think people don't see what's going on with you at home. When you don't manage anyone, you can hide behind your computer. But a manager has to show herself and share herself. Good managers have little room to hide.

Are you getting drunk every night? Are your finances a mess? You might have a fantasy that you are hiding bad behavior from coworkers, but stress shows up in nonverbal, unexpected ways that make people uncomfortable with you and worried about your competence. People who seem to have shaky lives at home seem like time bombs at work. So instead of trying to hide your personal life, redirect that energy toward improving your personal life. You might not have as much focus for work in the short term, but in the long term you'll be in better shape to manage effectively.

3. Manage hearts and minds. Sure, you need to manage budgets, schedules, and strategy, but if you don't have people's hearts on your side, your team won't overperform for you. The easiest way to win the hearts of your team members is to genuinely care about them. You can't fake this, so if you don't genuinely care about people who work for you, ask yourself why you are in management. There are plenty of big, rewarding careers that don't include management.

Management is about helping people be their best. Once you genuinely care about people, you will be able to find out what excites them, and you will help them reach their goals at work, which, invariably, will shine favorably on your own workplace performance.

4. *Manage diversity.* Study after study shows that diverse teams perform better than homogenous teams. And besides, diversity doesn't mean hiring someone in Mumbai. Managing diversity starts by hiring someone who is not like everyone else on your team. Then do it again and again and find a way to make the team gel.

Diverse teams are more difficult to manage—there are more opinions, more preconceptions, more quirks, and more conflicts. But top managers can leverage these difficulties as a means to establish more innovative planning. After all, no one ever became great by surrounding themselves with people who think like everyone else.

5. *Manage a successor.* Train someone to take over your job as soon as you have a handle on it yourself. That person should be practically doing your job so that you can find areas where you can take on different or larger responsibilities in the company. Managing a successor allows you to first lead without the title, and then to ask for the new title. And more money. Or, if it's your own company, managing a successor to your current duties is the key to being able to manage future growth yourself.

19. ASSUME THE JOB DESCRIPTION WAS WRONG

The best indicator of how people will act is how they have acted before. So you want to make sure that your first foray into management is a success. The majority of people who fail at their job will do so within the first ninety days. A big cause of failure during this time is that people are generally hired because of their skills and fired because of their personality.

When you are in management, personality matters more. For a nonmanager, skills matter more. This is a big contributor to managers failing so fast. So here are some steps you can take to make sure your interpersonal interactions do not lead you to management failure.

Have a vision. It might change, but you need to be able to tell people where you want to take them. The attributes of a leader are hard to muster if you don't know where you're going. And the best managers are actually leaders, on a small scale. People want to feel that they are working together toward a common, attractive goal that they can believe in. You need to convey this, even if you think it might change.

Your personality is tied, in people's minds, to what you have to offer. They will like you if they think you can do something for them. You cannot pretend to have vision and character if you don't, so figure it out fast, and then instead of blabbing about it to everyone in bombastic terms, trust that it will come out in your personality. And that people will be happy that you're there.

Assume everything in the interview was wrong. Don't come to work with a preconception of your job description. You'll be disappointed at best and annoyed at worst.

During the interview process, a hiring manager outlines a job description that will make you want to take the job. The description is not likely to be an accurate summary of what your boss really wants you to do. After all, no one says in an interview, "You'll have to pick up the pieces when my disorganization gets our team into trouble," or, "As a newcomer, you will take the projects no one else wants, which may or may not be relevant to your interests."

Also, during your initial meeting, you probably asked your prospective boss about his management style. The answer he gave was really the management style he thinks he *should* be using.

People do not generally say what they want. (This is so true that focus groups have to be run in a way that consumers are not directly asked what they want, because they say the wrong thing.) So watch your boss, read nonverbal cues, and understand what is motivating him or her. Once you truly understand your boss, you will be able to constantly adjust what you're doing in order to meet his or her needs.

Get your goals in writing. And meet them. Find out what your boss wants you to accomplish in the first ninety days. You need to know how you will be judged during this crucial time. Initiating this discussion shows that you are goal-oriented and you want to be part of your boss's agenda.

Ask for detailed descriptions and quantified expectations and get them in writing. Even if your boss does not create an official document, do it yourself in an e-mail—an informal summary of the conversation, but in your mind, treat this as a formal agreement.

In order to get past the first, tumultuous phase of your career life, you'll need to master management or recognize that you can't do it. Either conclusion is fine—self-knowledge is the important piece here. So take the task of being a new manager seriously because the results will show you where to go next.

II

How to Get What You Want from the People You Work With

Once you've figured out how to support yourself, the next step is to focus on getting what you want from work. The best way to do this is to be an extraordinary performer. This does not mean you should be the hardest worker. It means you should be absolutely clear on what your personal and professional goals are and use your skills to attain them. Stars at work get more feedback, more training, and better projects. Fortunately, you don't need the perfect job situation in order to be a star, because most star qualities you need will come from you—from taking your basically good skills and making them great.

Stars are different from everyone because of the strategies they use to perform their jobs and to work well with other people. It isn't so much what you're born with as how you use it. And the traits of star performers are traits you can teach yourself. Star strategies allow you to be highly effective, yet highly productive at the same time, so that you can fulfill your potential at work and in your personal life. Yes, stars have time for both.

To become your best self—a star, a great leader, a fulfilled worker—you need to know yourself and your goals very well. They probably don't include long hours at an office, and that's fine. Your goals include a mix of personal and professional aspirations, and that's fine, too. What Part Two will show you is how to create a new version of great that means great contribution, great ideas, great leadership, but not great sacrifice.

But you can't get any of this if you don't know what you want. Part of finding success in a career is knowing what it looks like to you. Part Two will teach you how to gain confidence in making decisions by giving you tips for being more honest with yourself about what your dreams are and what you value. Also, you'll need to surround yourself with people who will tell you candidly what you need to improve. Stars are great self-editors.

An important point of Part Two is that you are not in this world alone. Work is more fun if you like the people you work with and they like you. You'll get more of what you want for yourself if people like you, so Part Two coaches you on figuring out how likeable you are and how to get along with people even better. Being likeable to a wide range of people—your boss, your underlings, your customers—is a keystone to a great career.

Start now. It's a lifelong process, but if done honestly, it's the process that makes almost any job intrinsically challenging and interesting.

CHAPTER SEVEN

Playing Office Politics and Other Acts of Kindness

Here is a message for people who say they can't stomach office politics: you will die a slow, painful career death. That's because there's no getting around office politics, and mastering it is essential to being able to steer your own career because the out-of-office corollary to office politics is networking. And if you can't stomach networking, you'll have a lonely, isolated career in which no one is helping you.

Office politics is inescapable because it's about dealing with the people. When there is a group of people—anywhere, even on the playground—there is politics.

Let's say you pack up your bags and go work in a national park, with trees and rivers and no cubicles. There will be politics about who has to take care of hikers when it's raining and who gets to stay dry, and if you are bad at politics, you will be wet every time.

Politics is part of society. And my guess is that you want to participate in society (at least) so that you can support yourself.

If you think you hate office politics, think again. If you really take a look at what's going on over there at the water-cooler, people are not jockeying for power; they are hobnobbing for projects. That's right. For most people in today's workplace, office politics is about getting the best opportunities to learn and grow—the best projects, the best training, the best assignments to build skills and market value.

And networking is taking those ideas to the next level—making your talents known outside of your company, and even your industry. It is hard to fault people for wanting to grow and learn. In fact, I find more fault with people who care so little about personal growth that they won't spend the extra energy to learn to relate productively to other people.

Maybe you're convinced but are feeling at a loss for how to get started. This chapter will show you how to do the things that people who are good at office politics and networking do all the time:

1. *Make time for it.* Both in terms of face time and time alone to analyze the face time, you need to do this.
2. *Listen.* How can you learn anything when you're talking about what you already know?
3. *Have genuine interest in other people.* Each person is interesting if you are interested enough to ask the right questions.
4. *Feel empathy.* This means putting yourself in other people's shoes all the time. And not judging them.

Maybe you're still thinking of being the person at the office who abstains from office politics. Realize that you won't last long—in the office or in business. Putting your head down and doing your work is a good way to ensure that you don't connect with anyone. This situation is deadly in a world where people are hired for what they know and fired for who they are. People need to get to know you in order to like you.

The act of making yourself likeable and meeting new people is integral to your career. You shouldn't have to be fake if you are a geniuinely nice and interested person. If office politics and networking requires you to do something that feels fake, consider that you might not have been likeable in the first place.

For some people, office politics is a training ground for learning to be likeable, and as a side benefit, it will save their jobs. For others, office politics is the time at work when they get to be their best, true selves in search of more learning opportunities and more human connections.

20. BEING LIKEABLE MATTERS MORE THAN BEING COMPETENT

It's hard to underestimate the impact of good social skills on your career. In fact, across the board, in a wide variety of businesses, people would rather work with someone who is likeable and incompetent than with someone who is skilled and obnoxious, according to Tiziana Casciaro, professor at Harvard Business School. "How we value competence changes depending on whether we like someone or not," she says. People who lack social competence end up looking like they lack other competencies, too.

When it comes to holding down a job, social skills matter today more than ever. The only way to differentiate yourself at the bottom is to be likeable. As the need for social skills at work grows, the bar for good ones gets higher. Until the 1970s, a smart child uninterested in playground politics was considered eccentric but okay. Since the 1980s, educators see the playground as essential training for the future, and kids who can't navigate are often sent to experts for extra help with social skills.

Many people do not need to be taught to be likeable. But most of us have to work at it. Fortunately, Casciaro's research shows that the biggest impediment to likeability is not caring, so if you simply decide to do better, you probably will.

"Take responsibility for yourself," says executive coach Susan Hodgkinson. "Everyone needs to know that they are responsible for creating healthy, productive relationships at work." In other words, no one is going to make you likeable. Hodgkinson adds, "The people who are likeable actually care about other people and care about the connections they make."

Being good at talking to people requires that you figure out what interests them. For those who cannot master this, Casciaro recommends a tactical approach: "Find the hook that makes your similarities more visible. For example I might meet a man in his 60s and I'm a woman in my 30s but we both like basketball."

Also, figure out how to help someone else get what they need. "Recognize what you're trying to get done and who you are trying to get it done with. Then think beyond your own stuff to what the other people want," advises Hodgkinson. Think of this as project management synergy, or resume empathy; you need to help others reach their goals. This will make you more likeable and then more likely to reach your own goals.

And don't discount flattery. "Usually the reason we like someone is because we think they like us," says Casciaro. It's the rule of prom dates: he was ugly until he asked you to the prom, and now he doesn't look so bad. Since there is no prom at the office, she suggests "smiling and listening to make someone feel liked." Hodgkinson, however, cautions, "But it's not a personality popularity contest. You need to stay true to yourself while still expending empathy in order to connect."

So focus your energy on things that make you likeable—from how you talk to other people to how you talk to yourself. The next time you consider areas for self-improvement, choose interpersonal coaching over office skills and you'll likely get more bang for your buck.

21. MUD SLINGING MEANS YOU'RE LOSING GROUND

If you want people to like you, give them compliments. I know, that sounds like I'm telling you to brownnose. Actually, I'm telling you to find genuine ways to compliment people, which requires spending a lot of time looking for the good in people.

The difference between a genuine compliment and a brownnosing attempt is empathy and insight, according to Robert Kegan and Lisa Laskow Lahey, Harvard Graduate School of Education psychologists and coauthors of *How the Way We Talk Can Change the Way We Work: Seven Languages for Transformation.*

If you understand what worries someone, and what he is trying hardest to achieve personally, then you will easily spot opportunities for praise. Don't just say "good job" for the sake of it. In fact, don't just say "good job." The most effective compliments are very specific. And creative words are more memorable than standard words, according to Mark Knapp, communications professor at University of Texas. The most common types of praise are about possessions ("Nice car") or about actions ("Great shot").

But praise of character is the most rare and most memorable praise of all. It's also the most difficult because it requires you to understand the person you're praising and be thoughtful about how you talk to them. For example, "I appreciated the compassion you showed for the team when you were canceling the project."

To increase the weight of your compliments, establish yourself as a trusted resource. This means you need to be able to give people bad news as well as good news. I will never forget the employee who told me, "You know how everyone laughs at your jokes at the staff meeting? Well, the jokes are not that funny, but since all those people report to you, they laugh. You should stop with the jokes."

I was crushed to hear that I was not funny. But it would have been worse if I had been allowed to go on and on. (Though sometimes I tell myself that I really was funny and that particular employee just didn't get my humor.) And this person's subsequent compliments meant more to me because I knew she was honest.

Complimenting your boss is an important part of building a good relationship. Don't be shy because you have less experience. In fact, powerful people think that people who praise them are smarter and more likeable than those who don't, according to Knapp. On top of that, powerful people receive fewer compliments than the rest of us.

I never knew how important it is to compliment a boss until I complimented mine, mostly by accident. My boss gave a speech packed with bad news to employees, and I knew it had been hard for him. After the meeting, I stopped by his office to tell him privately, "You delivered the bad news really well. People were shocked, but they listened to you, and you made them hopeful."

His face brightened and he said, in a surprised voice, "Really?"

I realized immediately how much my input meant to him, how surprised he was to know I thought he did well, and how much he respected my assessment. I had thought he was too cocky for that. But that's the thing about complimenting your boss: it's disarming and makes your boss think of you as an equal.

To make a genuine connection, give genuine compliments, but balance them with insightful criticism. With the right balance, people will view you as a smarter person and they'll take all your comments more seriously.

So concentrate on the good in people and compliment it throughout the day. You just might feel like you're actually surrounded by kind, competent, and interesting people. And research shows that they will find you to be more kind and competent as well.

22. FORGET 360-DEGREE REVIEWS, GO TO COUPLES THERAPY INSTEAD

Couples therapy: my husband is slumped at the edge of the sofa, sulking. I sit in the center cushion, upright and animated, ranting about why he needs to get rid of his bike.

The therapist tells me to be quiet, but in that couples-therapist way: "Let's give him a chance to talk about the bike." My husband says he needs to keep the bike in the kitchen, where it will stay until he formulates a daily riding schedule.

I listen. But not really. Mostly I plan my arguments about why what he is saying is irrelevant and why I am right.

My husband is so concerned about planning everything that he cannot actually execute a plan. So I know the bike will be in the kitchen forever. Unlike my husband, I have no patience for details, and I *always* have a plan. When we decided to have a child, he wanted to overcome every hurdle first—from finding an apartment with a playroom to setting up a college fund. I told him we had to move forward, hurdles and all.

Our therapist has tried a lot of tactics to get us to communicate. I finally took notice when she observed that the problems I have in talking to my husband are probably the same types of problems I have in talking to people at work. This made sense to me immediately because I always say that I love my husband but would never want to work with someone like him.

He's a slow, methodical thinker, and I generally do not have patience for people like him at work. But the therapist pointed out that I chose such a person for a husband. "You must have had a reason," she said. And it's true. In my heart of hearts, I know that a slow, methodical thinker is the perfect counterpoint for me—in my personal and professional life.

My therapist was talking about the importance of understanding personality types. Personality testing has a strong foothold in corporate life as a way to pinpoint difficulties and solve them. "If someone is annoying or difficult to communicate with, usually there are fundamental personality type differences between the two people," says Rob Toomey of SpeedReading People.

I have spent a lot of time reading about the Myers-Briggs personality test, which is why I understand my personality type and my husband's. A good place to start, if you want to understand these types, is *Do What You Are,* by Paul Tieger and Barbara Barron-Tieger. Once you understand your personality type you'll better understand your strengths and weaknesses. And, as you read about the other personality types, you'll better understand how to work more effectively with others.

I took the Myers-Briggs test a few times before I believed my results, and then I felt compelled to read about everyone's personality, not just mine, in order to figure out who I am by understanding who I am not.

Knowing what to change about your personality traits and making the changes are two distinct steps. This is another situation in which it's good to have a significant other to give you a kick in the pants. For example, often when someone (including my husband) is talking to me, I seem as though I'm listening, but in reality I'm more interested in my own ideas than those of the person talking. I talk over and past them. I am dismissive and unresponsive. "How do you keep people from strangling you?" my husband asks when he's particularly annoyed and probably considering strangling me himself. He has helped me realize that I have personality traits that make me unproductive—at work and at home.

So back to the bike. I tell myself that if I'm patient, he'll come up with a great plan that will make keeping the bike in the apartment a good idea. That if I can just learn to control myself in the context of the bike, the therapist, and the annoyed husband, then I will do much better in my career. It is clear to me that I deal with my husband in the same way as I deal with people at work. And my career will be stronger if I can become a stronger marriage partner, because the communication skills are the same.

So every time I get frustrated in couples therapy, or I think that it's a waste of money, I remind myself that communication skills know no boundaries. I can tell myself that I'm a good communicator at work, but the best feedback I can get is at home. If you want to know what your weak points are at work, and why you may not be getting along with certain coworkers, ask your significant other— that person knows.

And if you want to make a lot of headway in terms of having your personality mesh with other people's, take a look at yourself, through the eyes of Myers-Briggs or some other personality test. Then train yourself to quickly read what type of personality is sitting across from you. It's a skill that takes years and years to master, but as someone who has spent years and years and still hasn't mastered it, I can tell you that every ounce of improvement in the areas of understanding personality types will help you get along better with people.

23. BLAME YOURSELF FIRST

When you have a problem with how other people in the office are treating you, figure out how *you* can change. When you have a problem with how people want you to do your job, change *your* approach, or change *your* job description, but don't blame others for what they want; that won't get you anywhere.

Your success depends on your ability to get control of a problem and solve it. So think about yourself first. This might sound harsh, but it's actually very optimistic: if you blame yourself for bad situations, you will be happier in life.

Social psychologists have found that people differ with regard to how much control they feel they have over their lives. People with an "internal locus of control" believe they act by choice, while those with an "external locus of control" believe they are unduly controlled by fate, the political structure, and other external sources. People with a high internal locus of control believe their success is caused by intrinsic factors, are more achievement-oriented and self-confident, are less anxious, suspicious, and dogmatic, and tend to be better adjusted than those with a high external locus of control.

You need to be a person who fixes what's wrong in your life instead of complaining about it. But you can't do everything yourself, and great problem solvers usually have great coaches. Most of your problems in life will stem from the same set of weaknesses. Maybe it'll be that you're really sensitive, or you have no patience, or you think people don't listen to you. Weaknesses are hard to beat. Actually, Martin Seligman, professor of psychology at the University of Pennsylvania, says that instead of focusing on overcoming weaknesses, we should focus on strengths. Finding core strengths is difficult but a coach can help you do that and then use those strengths to overcome problems.

I am a big fan of career coaches and life coaches, but be careful, because a good coach is hard to find. I learned to find good coaches by enduring bad ones. I also learned that when you find a good one, you can change in ways that will surprise you.

The first career coach I ever hired was someone my boss recommended. He gave me the guy's phone number and I called. The coach's voice mail message closed with, "Have a wonderful and life-changing day!" I told my boss I could not work with someone who was so annoyingly positive.

My boss said, "This guy is renowned for working with famous businesswomen." (My boss dropped the name of a woman who worked with this coach. To this day I still question her judgment.) I wanted to be famous, so I agreed to meet with the guy.

He told me that most women he worked with needed to learn to be more assertive. He said, "I can tell you would be responsive to that sort of training because you're wearing a skirt." Then he winked at me. In a move of assertiveness, I fired him.

My second coach was someone my boss read about in a newsletter. This coach told me I needed to appear grounded and stable as a leader. His observation hit a nerve: I had catapulted to the number-two position in my company, and some days I wondered what I was doing there. I thought

I was wondering privately, but the coach showed me how my demeanor gave it away. "You walk like you're on air," he told me. "Your bounce denotes giddiness and your swinging arms look impetuous."

He showed me how to walk so that I looked grounded and stable: less arm movement, less bounce in my knees, a shorter gait. We also worked on how I breathed as I walked. I relaxed my diaphragm and took deeper breaths, which actually shifted my weight more toward the ground. The most interesting thing he taught me was that if I could change how I walk, I would change how I felt. I didn't believe it until he forced me to try it.

Later I saw a coach speaking at an entrepreneurs' conference. I hired her to help me handle board meetings. She recognized that one of my strengths was communication, and we worked on making it better. She taught me not to smile so much. She pointed out that women smile a lot and men don't and it makes men nervous. To soften the blow, she smiled at me. She also told me my sweater was cut a little low for making a first impression of seriousness. By focusing on a strength—public speaking—she taught me skills to overcome problems such as sexual discrimination and nerves.

When it comes to choosing a coach, interview a few because each coach has a different approach, and not all will be right for you. To get a sense of the coach, ask, "What are you best at doing with your clients?" If you like the answer, do a short trial session. If you ask people what they're best at and they won't give a specific answer, or they say they do everything, it's probably because they're not good at anything, so hang up.

Recommendations from a respected friend or coworker are good bets. But, as you can see from my experience, a recommendation isn't foolproof. I have had good luck going to a bookstore and perusing the careers section for books by coaches. If you like a book, you will probably like the coach who wrote it. Many coaches speak at conferences, so go to listen to a few if you're on the prowl. Another good resource is the career coach hotline: www .careercoachhotline.com.

Enlisting the help of a coach may seem extreme—it's another expense, plus it takes time and energy to find a good one. But people who succeed in getting what they want out of life can point to people who helped guide them. You can wait around for decades until that person comes into your life, or you can get moving right away and hire someone who can coach you toward your strengths. The faster you know how to be your most likeable self at work, the faster you'll be able to set up the best life for yourself.

CHAPTER EIGHT

Authenticity Is the Buzzword of the New Millennium

I went on a business trip and I took my mom. When I got there it was apparent that I was underdressed, so we went shopping. I planned on getting rid of my ratty sneakers, but my mom said I needed a suit. Somehow a civilized disagreement turned into an all-out fight with both of us using clothing as a metaphor for everything we hate about each other. At some point, I said under my breath, "I'm going to write about this."

My mom said, "Don't do that! You'll make yourself look bad! People will know you didn't dress properly."

But here it is, for the world to know: I dressed inappropriately! I ended up buying expensive shoes that I already had at home! And I fought with my mom in public!

Surely you've had a moment of failing—maybe similar to this one. Don't be so quick to hide it from people, because the new battleground in business is authenticity and you'd better get some.

The *Harvard Business Review* reports that authenticity is the trait that uniquely defines great leaders. Generation Y values authenticity above almost everything else, according to reports from the demographic research firm Yankelovich Partners.

The power of authenticity hit me recently, when I had a speaking engagement at the Richard Ivey School of Business in London, Ontario. In a post-event survey, the reaction of the students was very positive. Ironically, though, it wasn't the content of the speech they cited so much as the authenticity.

Research published in the *Harvard Business Review* explains that authenticity is largely defined by what other people see in you. So you have a good amount of control over how authentic you appear.

Being genuine means you don't do or say things you don't believe. Everyone understands this in principle. But people who are authentic are fanatical about it. The other quality you need for authenticity is to be able to relate to a lot of types of people—otherwise you'll have a career in which you only connect to people who are like you.

The first thing, then, is to know who you are and what you believe. Then you need to have confidence that being your true self will get you where you want to go. Manage your authenticity by only revealing the parts of you that will best connect with your audience.

Success at work requires working well with many different types of people while remaining true to yourself. You do not have to agree with everything your boss does, for example. But you have to speak about his policies in ways that remain true to your own values—which means not lying, but not undermining your boss, either. People who think this task is impossible are, in my mind, people who are too lazy to be authentic.

The real work of authenticity is not just knowing yourself, but taking the time to understand where other people are coming from and to respect them for that. If you have a fur coat and you love skiing, talk to the animal rights activist about skiing and talk to the seventy-year-old heiress about fur coats. In both cases you can be authentic without putting the other person off.

A lot of people think that the business world is not compatible with authenticity. However, the exact opposite is true: those who stand out as leaders have a notable authenticity. People are attracted to this quality because the alternative is so disappointing—clichéd relationships, empty promises, and conversation with no soul. What people value in business is what they value in all of life, and that is a real connection. People need to see a genuine part of you and they need to relate to it. So, in many cases, a wardrobe mishap or fight with your mom is a good opening.

This chapter will show you the convoluted ways you undermine your authenticity and what you can do to help yourself. Everything you do—talking, writing, eating—is an opportunity to be more authentic, so don't blow it.

24. THE DIFFERENCE BETWEEN FEAR AND EXCITEMENT IS BREATHING

My cousin had a karaoke party. I had to go because he's my cousin, but I refused to sing because this would have pained the audience even more than it would have pained me. A woman at the party, however, impressed me by engaging the crowd even though she had no apparent singing talent. I wanted this: I wanted to be able to make people want to listen to me.

So I did something that I fantasize about a lot but rarely do with any competence: I made a great business connection at a party. It turned out that this woman, Lindy, is a Sanford Meisner–trained actress who works for a consulting firm teaching executives how to strengthen business relationships by using acting techniques. Lindy Amos would never say she teaches public speaking skills, even though I would say that. Lindy would say she teaches people to build connections through authenticity, which is what you should aim for in public speaking. I signed up.

At our first session, Lindy explained the premise: acting and leading are both about establishing a relationship with an audience and making them believe in you. My first assignment was to memorize a short speech—"Ain't I a Woman," by Sojourner Truth. I loved the speech but I hated having to memorize it, and I dreaded having to recite it in front of Lindy. Then I remembered what Lindy's boss said at the beginning of the course: this program is best suited to high-level executives with enough self-confidence to explore leadership techniques that might feel silly at first. I wanted to fit into this self-confident high-level executive category, so I forced myself to show up for the second meeting.

I bombed. I couldn't remember the speech. Lindy told me to think less about the speech and more about connecting with her, my audience. Finally, when I looked at her the way I look at my husband when I need him to pick up the dry cleaning, she was satisfied. I may have gotten the look down, but my delivery was still off. Lindy instructed me to reengage her whenever I sensed I was losing her. I started over. She stopped me immediately. "You can't just start over," she said. "Leaders stick with their audience and fight to get them back." "How do I do that?" I asked. "Take a risk," she said. In acting, you might ad-lib; in business, you can ask a rhetorical question. So I did, and then started talking right away. She pointed out that a good leader is comfortable with a long pause, which shows trust that the audience is thinking. Speaking too fast doesn't allow the audience to absorb or interpret, killing any chance of making a connection.

My biggest problem, according to Lindy, was wanting to appear like a cool and hip leader and not paying attention to my audience. I made it about me instead of about them. "Pretend you're an evangelist preacher," she said, because preachers excel at engaging listeners. I continued to give my speech, adding after every few sentences, "Can I get an 'Amen'?" I felt more and more pathetic as Lindy sat in stony silence, ignoring my bleating pleas. Then I realized that if I didn't care about what I was saying, no one else would. You really have to want an "Amen" to get one, and finally I did.

After this breakthrough, the sessions became easier. The principles of theater and management are the same: a director and a manager both have to lead in ways that allow for and encourage a person's best, most creative self. Managing is about performing, which takes practice, energy, and concentration. The basics are these: Believe your material. Know your audience. Engage them so they are invested in what you have to say. And for those of you who are not yet managers, *acting* like a manager is the first step toward becoming one.

When I realized how difficult it is to master Lindy's idea of making a connection, I asked her for things I can do at home. Here are some suggestions she had:

1. *Read out loud, slowly, for five minutes a day.* I talk quickly, and this is not a way to project authenticity and a heartfelt effort at communication.

2. *Practice telling stories.* This is something we are more comfortable with than, say, giving a speech or going to a difficult meeting. But if we get practice being our true self while telling a story, authenticity will come more naturally when talking about something more difficult.

3. *Practice deep breathing.* Lindy told me an American Indian proverb: "The difference between fear and excitement is breathing." She said, "Fear causes your breathing to become shallow, your muscles to tense, and your brain to go blank. We communicate to have impact. If we're not breathing, we're not even present. There is no chance of having impact if you aren't even present. Deep breaths free your constricted chest, oxygenate your blood, and put you in charge of your brain again."

Lindy is consumed with the idea that the way to get people to listen to you is to sound authentic. This is true whether you are talking to someone one-on-one in an elevator or talking to a thousand people in an auditorium. So you have to find your authentic self: know what you are passionate about. What is really driving you to talk about what you talk about? Understanding your personal motivations is the first step toward projecting your authentic self. You will change throughout the years, but the practice of projecting who you really are will not change, once you learn how to do it.

25. STOP USING ADVERBS

If you want people to pay attention to what you have to say, write short. This is true in all of life, but most true at work. Most of the writing we do at work is in the format of an e-mail, proposal, or presentation—all documents that your audience wants to get through quickly. The faster and more concisely you get to your point, the more likely your reader will stick with you and understand your message. "If today the president got up and addressed the nation in 270 words, it'd be a top news story. People will pay more attention because you're so brief," writes Janice Obuchowski in the *Harvard Management Update*.

We sound most authentic when we talk, and verbally, short, simple sentence construction comes naturally to us. When we write, authenticity gets buried under poor word choice. For example, people who use complicated words are seen as not as smart as people who write with a more basic vocabulary. "It's important to point out that this research is not about problems with using long words but about using long words needlessly," says Daniel Oppenheimer, professor of psychology at Princeton University.

Writing short is not easy. Take the 270-word Gettysburg Address, for example. "Lincoln didn't just suddenly master elegant language. He wrote wonderful, down to earth language that was very concrete. But he rigorously trained himself to do that," says Bryan Garner, editor of *A Dictionary of Modern American Usage*.

Here are some self-editing tricks for writing shorter:

1. Write lists. People love reading lists. They are faster and easier to read than unformatted writing, and they are more fun. If you can't list your ideas, then you aren't organized enough to send them to someone else.

2. Think on your own time. Most of us think while we write. But people don't want to read your thinking process; they want to see the final result. Find your main point in each paragraph and delete everything else. If someone is dying to know your logic, they'll ask.

3. Keep paragraphs short. Your idea gets lost in a paragraph that's more than four or five lines. Two lines is the best length if you really need your reader to digest each word.

4. Write like you talk. Each of us has the gift of rhythm when it comes to sentences, which includes a natural economy of language. But you must practice writing in order to transfer your verbal gifts to the page. Start by avoiding words you never say. For example, you would never say "in conclusion" when you are speaking to someone so don't use it when you write.

5. Delete. When you're finished, you're not finished: cut 10 percent of the words. I do this with every column I write. Sometimes, in fact, I realize that I can cut 25 percent of the words, and then my word count isn't high enough to be a column and I have to think of more things to say. Luckily, you don't have to write for publication, so you can celebrate if you cut more than 10 percent. (Note: it is cheating to do this step before you really think you're done.)

6. *Avoid telltale signs of a rube.* Passive voice. Almost no one ever speaks this way. And on top of that, when you write in it you give away that you are unclear about who is doing what, because the nature of the passive voice is to obscure the person taking the action. Check yourself: search for all instances of "by" in your document. If you have a noun directly after "by" then it's passive voice. Change it.

7. *Avoid adjectives and adverbs.* The fastest way to a point is to let the facts speak for themselves. Adjectives and adverbs are your interpretation of the facts. If you present the right facts, you won't need to throw in your interpretation. For example, you can write, "Susie's project is going slowly." Or you can write, "Susie's project is behind schedule." If you use the first sentence, you'll have to use the second sentence, too, but the second sentence encompasses the first. So as you cut your adjectives and adverbs, you might even be able to cut all the sentences that contain them.

I just checked to see if I have modifiers in this section. I do, but I think I use them well. You will think this, too, about your own modifiers when you go back over your writing. But I have an editor and you don't, and I usually use a modifier to be funny, while you do not need to be funny in professional e-mails. So get rid of your adverbs and adjectives, really.

26. LEVERAGE YOUR CORE COMPETENCIES BY OFF-LOADING JARGON

Don't use jargon. I know you've heard this before, but maybe no one has ever told you the real reason for the rule. You lose your authenticity when you reach for clichéd phrases, and your choice of jargon reveals your weakness. Today business writing is "mired in cliché. It's very stiff, striving to impress. It's not honest: Here's who I am," says Tim Schellhardt, former bureau chief at the *Wall Street Journal* and now a public relations executive.

Phrases like "leverage your core competencies" spread through corporate life because the pressure to conform at work can be intense. Once you hear other people using the jargon, it's easy to use it yourself. The result is an environment in which no voice stands out as authentic, according to Brian Fugere, Chelsea Hardaway, and Jon Warshawsky, authors of *Why Business People Speak Like Idiots: A Bullfighter's Guide.*

There's also jargon that cuts across most industries— the phrases you hear whether you're an accountant in consumer products or a programmer in health care. Most people understand this jargon, but using it makes you look bad because most cross-industry jargon is a euphemism for being desperate or incompetent or calling someone else desperate or incompetent. Here are some examples:

- *Let's think out of the box.* "Can you creatively anemic people please come up with something?" People who really do think out of the box do it whether they are told to or not. That's how they think. If you feel like you need to tell someone to think out of the box, then it's probably hopeless. The person who says, "Let's think out of the box" is usually desperate for a new idea and surrounded by people who are not known for generating them. So the phrase is actually an announcement that says, "I'm in trouble."

- *I need someone who can hit the ground running.* "I am screwed." No one can hit the ground running. You need to at least assess what race you're in and who else is running. Everyone has a race strategy when they are in the blocks. You need a little time to get one. In the case of a new hire, this means taking some time to assess company politics. If your employer needs you to hit the ground running, then you've already missed your window to achieve success.

- *Let's hit a home run.* "I'm desperate to look good. Even though the odds of a home run are slim, I'm banking on one because it's the only thing that'll save me." Here's something for all you sports fans to remember: if you have a bunch of solid hitters, you don't need a bunch of home runs.

- *You and I are not on the same page.* "Get on my page. Your page is misguided." No one ever says, "We're not on the same page, so let me work really hard to understand your point of view." If you want to understand someone else, you say, "Can you tell me more about how you're thinking."

- *I'm calling to touch base.* "I want something from you but I can't say it up front." Or, "I am worried that you are lost and I'm sniffing around for signs to confirm my hunch." Or, "I'm calling because you micromanage me."

- *My plate is full.* "Help I'm drowning." Or, "I would kill myself before I'd work on your project."
- *Let's close the loop.* "Let me make sure I'm not going to get into trouble for this one."
- *Let's touch base next week.* "I don't want to talk to you now." Or, "You are on a short leash and you need to report back to me."
- *Keep this on your radar.* "This will come back to bite you…or me."

I sent this list to Peter Degen-Portnoy, president of Innovatium, and he pointed out one I missed: "We're not communicating well" means "I don't like you."

I have never met Peter in person, but he sends me smart and soul-searching e-mails that reveal an authenticity that makes me feel like we're friends. He never uses jargon, at least with me. So I like him.

Those of you who strive to be authentic every day of your life will not be derailed by jargon. For those who are connected to their work and their coworkers, jargon will not feel appropriate, so you'll rarely use it. Use jargon as a sign that you are disconnected to whatever is going on that is related to the jargon. If you treat the disconnectedness, and reestablish authenticity, the jargon will go away.

CHAPTER NINE

Sex Discrimination Is Everywhere, So Don't Try to Run

The best way to deal with sex discrimination is to be clear about what's going on and then do your best to ignore it. This is true for men and women. This is not "the women's chapter." This is the chapter for everyone who is concerned about any kind of discrimination at work. Here are some studies to sink your teeth into:

- When men are in the hiring position, women are likely to be penalized for negotiating for a higher starting salary and men are not. (Carnegie Mellon University, 2005)
- Women with children get hired at lower salaries than people without children. Men with children get hired at salaries higher than people without children and women with children. (Cornell University, 2005)
- When women start to dominate a field, the salaries go down. Average pay in human resources, for example,

has gone down 20 percent since women took over. (CNN.com)

■ Women scientists at MIT receive less pay, space, and rewards than male scientists. (MIT)

I do not believe these examples of discrimination are intentional. I believe they are true, but I also believe that most people who participated in this discrimination wish they hadn't. There are a few benefits to holding this belief. First, I can continue working within a flawed system (very flawed). Second, I do not feel the need to attack every person who flagrantly discriminates against me or in front of me (which is often). Third, I get to feel forgiving, and forgiving someone is an important part of ensuring that discrimination does not harm your soul. (The twenty or so studies that support this last point say that people who forgive are most capable of being happy, and forgiveness might actually promote happiness.)

I am not way off base in my forgiving attitude, though. In a survey of college students, the majority of male students who harassed female students were surprised to hear that the women did not think it was funny. The men just thought they were making a joke. One of the most notable trends among people entering the workforce is their tolerance and sense of inclusiveness. These are people who were raised to be tolerant. Discrimination is not gone, but today more than ever, it is widely thought of as unacceptable. The persistent problem is that we all discriminate unconsciously. Even me: the first time I was in a position to hire my own team, I hired only men. I knew intuitively that women look more powerful managing men than managing women, and I wanted to look good. I didn't do it consciously—I only realized years later what had been going on.

While it's always horrible when it happens, often discrimination is subtle and unintentional. And often, attacking the person instead of forgiving their ignorance is not the best course of action in the workplace. Sometimes you can actually turn the tables and use the harassment to better your career. You can choose to dedicate your life to ending discrimination, but instead of kicking and screaming at work—and probably killing your ability to earn a living—you might consider starting with yourself instead of your office. Whether we want to admit it or not, we all hold some discriminatory views. Deal with those to make the world a better place, instead of trying to change the way the people at your office think.

Of course, not all discrimination is subtle and unintentional. Some of it is violent, and you should use the law to squelch that. Some is institutional—starting in the CEO's office and trickling down the ranks, protected by human resources—and you should stay away from that. This chapter gives specific advice for specific situations. But keep in mind the flight attendant's instructions to put your own air mask on before helping your child: you can't save the world until you save yourself.

27. A LAWSUIT WILL HURT YOU WORSE THAN HARASSMENT

Sexual harassment in American work life is pervasive—as much as 80 percent in certain sectors, according to one study. But most women don't stand a chance of winning a lawsuit. So having a plan to deal with the problem is a good idea for all women.

When it comes to harassment, many women report that they choose to confront the offender rather than report the problem formally to human resources.

You might think about taking that approach as well. Most harassment isn't severe enough to hold up in court, and the law isn't strong enough to protect you from most types of retaliation. So unless your safety is at risk, you're often better off handling the harasser yourself rather than reporting him to human resources.

To win a lawsuit, courts require proof that harassment was severe and pervasive in the work environment, according to employment lawyer Alisa Epstein. And that employee handbook becomes important, too. Yet most employees have never read their handbook, and if they have, they may not have done so as carefully as they need to.

When you report harassment to human resources, you must follow your company's policy precisely or you risk losing your ability to take the company to court.

After you've filed a report, human resources will protect the company, not you. Human resource executives talk about their concern for harassment. But according to employment lawyer Jim Weliky, "Most HR departments don't live up to their propaganda."

The law is set up to encourage a company to take pro-scribed steps to protect itself from liability rather than to protect your emotional stability, or for that matter, your career.

Once you take action against a harasser, retaliation is your biggest problem. "Very few retaliation cases we have were not triggered by reporting the problem to human resources," says Weliky. "But not all retaliation is strong enough to make it to court."

Retaliation is usually subtle: fewer invitations to lunch, a cubicle that isolates you from office networks, and project assignments that are boring. That sort of retaliation effec-tively holds back your career without standing up in court.

Just because you don't have a lawsuit doesn't mean you need to put up with harassment or retaliation. It means you need to take things into your own hands.

Your goal should be to stop the harassment without hurting your career. No small feat but possible.

"This is a negotiable moment," says Carol Froh-linger, attorney and author of *Her Place at the Table: A Woman's Guide to Negotiating Five Key Challenges to Leadership Success.* "Before going to human resources, have a frank conversation with the person making you uncomfortable."

Be clear on what behavior is harassing and that you don't like it.

"As long as he doesn't repeatedly refuse to negotiate like saying, 'You're so premenstrual' and walking away," Froh-linger said, "you should negotiate things for yourself."

As in any important negotiating session Frohlinger advises that you assess your "best alternative to a negotiated agreement," or BATNA.

Your BATNA is probably to leave the company. But you should let your opponent feel that your BATNA is to go to human resources, because no matter how arrogant he is, he will not be happy about being dragged into a "he said–she said" mess before the human resources department.

When you negotiate, aim high: if your harasser is your boss, ask for help to switch departments, and ask to go to a better department with a top manager. It's in your harasser's interest to help you. Or, if a coworker is harassing you, make sure the coworker appreciates that you handled things yourself. You save the coworker a lot of problems by not reporting him.

These are ways to decrease the chances of retribution while squelching the harassing behavior.

If the harasser will not negotiate with you, assess your power versus his. "Sexual harassment is more about the balance of power than what has been said," says Weliky.

Kate, a high-powered New York City lawyer, recalls an incident when she was young and working with a managing director. He told her, "Bring the papers by my hotel room, and don't worry if I'm only wearing a towel."

She thought the comment was ludicrous and told the whole office. "I could do that because I was on my way up in that firm and he was doing poorly," she said. "He didn't have a lot of ways to make my life difficult. In fact, someone told his wife and she bawled him out in front of his coworkers."

A great situation, but most of you cannot depend on your harasser's wife for vigilante law enforcement.

If the balance of power is not in your favor, and you get nowhere negotiating, you should consider finding a new job and leaving the offending company—in that order, because it's always easier to find a job when you have a job, even if you hate the job you have.

There is plenty to do in this world that does not require you to work in companies that enable a boys' club atmosphere. There are a lot of men who feel alienated in this atmosphere, too. Find those men and work with them. Then get a lot of power in your career and create a workplace culture you believe in.

28. USE HARASSMENT TO BOOST YOUR CAREER

Each time in my career that I have ignored sexual harassment aimed at me, I have moved up the corporate ladder. For example, the boss who once pulled all senior management out of the company's sexual harassment seminar because he thought it was a waste of time—and patted me on the butt as he left the room—has turned out to be my most reliable cheerleader (and a very impressive reference).

In the first eight days of my job at a financial software company, I was sexually harassed six times by my new boss. This list does not include his sexual harassment of me during the interview process, which I chose to ignore because it was my first interview at a respectable company in six months.

Maybe you're wondering what, exactly, I regard as sexual harassment. The easiest conversation to relay is this one:

Me: "Thank you for setting up that meeting; it will be very helpful."

Boss: "Big testicles." (He then pretends to squeeze his genitals.)

I had no idea what he meant by this comment, but it is a short and easy way to make my case.

Here's another choice moment: When he took me out for lunch on my second day on the job, he told me he once fell in love with a woman as tall as I am but was intimidated by her height, so they just had casual sex. I said nothing in response.

I knew, though, from a legal perspective (and also a moral one) that I needed to tell him his comments were unwanted. So that afternoon when he said, "I want to hug you, but it would be illegal," I said, "You're right."

Each night, I relayed some of the best lines from work to my husband. He was stunned. He couldn't believe these events actually happened in today's workplaces. I told him this was standard. He told me I should sue so that we could go to Tahiti. I told him if I sued, I'd probably settle out of court after three years for about $200,000, and I'd be a pariah in the workplace.

I told my husband that his very hot, twenty-seven-year-old boss gets hit on as much as I do. He insisted it didn't happen. I told him he wouldn't know because *of course* men don't harass women in front of other men. After all, it's illegal. I suggested to my husband that he was perpetuating the myth that harassment isn't widespread.

In fact, 44 percent of women between ages thirty-five and forty-nine report experiencing sexual harassment at the workplace—even though almost every company has an explicit no-tolerance policy. A national survey shows that 21 percent of *all* women report being sexually harassed at work, while a Rutgers University study indicates that for knowledge-based workers, the percentage can go as high as 88 percent. Yet when women leverage the no-tolerance policy, their names are plastered over the business pages and they are blacklisted in their industry.

Often the best way to change corporate America is from within: gain a foothold and then wield your power. To get power, you have to stay in the workforce, not the court system, and make yourself highly valued. Unfortunately, this means learning how to navigate a discriminatory system. But when you know the system, you are then clear about the root of its problems, and you know how to initiate change.

In this spirit, I hatched a plan to rid myself of my harassing boss. I knew that management was smart and that if I explained why I wanted to be moved to another department, they would see my request as extremely reasonable. I figured they would be grateful for my low-key approach to this sensitive problem, rather than resentful that I had been hired to work in business development and yet was asking to be switched to a department with no openings.

I was right. I was moved into marketing, which I prefer. I received a more prestigious assignment and gained a smarter boss. If I reported that I'd been sexually harassed during the interview process, I would not have gotten the job. Had I reported the harassment to my boss's boss without presenting a plan for solving the problem, I would not have received a better assignment. If you have a strategy, enduring sexual harassment can sometimes be a way to gain power to achieve your long-range goals.

Each situation is different, but if you know what you want from your career, then you may see harassment as a way to meet those goals—to take a horrible situation and get something positive out of it. Once the company or a boss is in a compromised position because of harassment, you are in a position to ask for a little bit more than you'd normally get.

As with all opportunities in life, you do not have an opportunity if you don't have a goal. Although I didn't like my boss, I did like the company, and I knew I wanted

to be in a different department, so I jumped at the chance
to get there. Be creative. Since harassment is illegal (and
wrong)—and even my absurd boss, I'm sure, was not
being an idiot intentionally—people may be responsive to
reasonable requests. A reasonable request shows that you
are committed to growing within the company and that
you will not create a storm with the harassment claim as
long as the situation is remedied. Your goals should be
to stop the harassment and get to a good spot. You can
often achieve this without retribution, pomp and circumstance, or outrage. It all goes back to forgiveness, and your
happiness, of course.

29. DON'T BE SUPPORTIVE

It's time for a new approach to squelching the gender-wage gap and getting more women into senior management. For one thing, today's wage gap doesn't begin until women are in the middle of their career, according to the Catalyst Group. A big contributor to this statistic is women cutting back on work to raise children. But another contributing factor, Catalyst reports, is the tendency of women to choose support roles rather than line manager positions.

Don't know the difference between the two types of jobs? Line managers are directly responsible for generating money for the company (think: product management, sales). Support staff is responsible for making things run smoothly so the line managers can generate money (think: human resources, public relations, customer service).

While men often shoot themselves to the stars as line managers, women get to middle management as support staff and find their career in a black hole. This pattern leaves women with stagnant salaries and companies with no women in senior management. When you're planning your career, set yourself up for a line position. (This advice applies to men, too, though they seem to steer away from support roles instinctively.)

Think about all the CEOs who worked their way up the ranks; you'll be hard-pressed to come up with someone who made her mark on the company in a support role. When a company blows Wall Street away with amazing revenues, does anyone give customer service credit? No. Does anyone ask PR managers for their opinions on company earnings? No. (In fact, PR managers often get fired for giving their own opinion.) The only time anyone interviews HR managers is when line managers need help getting jobs.

Most support roles are dead-end career paths—they end in middle management with no place else to go. Support managers don't have the profit-and-loss experience necessary for a senior management position. But you never hear someone say a line manager doesn't have the support experience necessary for a senior job. That's because every line manager has to deal with people on a daily basis.

Women often end up in support departments because they think of themselves as being "good with people." And then a terrible career adviser says something like, "How about public relations? You can talk to people all day!" But you know what? Telephone operators have to be good with people, too—that doesn't mean you should aspire to that job.

In fact, being good with people is an essential trait for managers in all areas of a company. If you think you're good with people, then you are a great candidate for senior management. So put yourself on the senior management track by aiming for profit-and-loss responsibilities.

If you're a college student, be careful to interview only for jobs in departments led by line managers. If you're already in the workforce and you're in a support role, do everything you can to move into another department. Take a pay cut if you have to—you'll more than make that money back in the middle of your career when you still have room to move up the corporate ladder.

CHAPTER TEN

Electronic Communication Cannot Enhance Relationships You Don't Have

The media talks a lot about information overload, but young workers are comfortable with a deluge of information. Most twentysomething workers look at computers all day, and IM their friends at night. The technology issues they face are how to combat cubicle alienation and how to use e-mail effectively in the workplace.

Jose Olivo, for example, is a desktop analyst, which means, in many cases, when someone's computer has a problem, Olivo fixes it while the person goes to lunch. Other times, Olivo works on someone's computer remotely, without leaving his desk. This is all highly efficient, but completely lacking in social opportunity.

Everyone's day should include "human moments," a term coined by Edward M. Hallowell, a psychiatrist and senior lecturer at Harvard Medical School. He writes that the human moment is "an authentic psychological encounter that can happen only when two people share the same physical space. It has two prerequisites: people's physical presence and their emotional and intellectual attention."

The need to have regular human moments during the workday is similar to the need to stand up and stretch on the airplane: your well-being depends on it. Even if your office is a coffee shop at the end of your block, those frequent trips to the barista provide a nice face-to-face moment if you make a bit of small talk.

In a large company, office politics is mostly office networking, and the people who are doing it best are doing it in person. In person, you get nonverbal information about someone that you can't get through e-mail. And that person gets information about you, too. The connection is more informative just because it's in person.

Some people who use technology for almost all communication are actually dodging face-to-face life because it's too difficult. For an introvert, technology is a social godsend, but relying on it too much will undermine your good work at the office: no one will know who you are.

Technology is only part of your communication repertoire. Use it well, but use it with caution. The younger generations have a lock on technological communication and the older generations often scoff at overreliance on technology. The people who can bridge gaps between the two types of communication will stand out in a multigenerational office.

30. DOES YOUR E-MAIL MAKE YOU LOOK BAD? TAKE THE TEST

You cannot be organized if your e-mail is not organized. If you cannot keep up with your e-mail, then you scream to people that you're overwhelmed with your job, and maybe your life (depending on how many personal e-mails you get and do not answer). Don't tell me you get too much e-mail. Everyone gets too much e-mail. You still need to be able to deal with it effectively.

If you answer yes to any of these three questions, you need to get a better grip on your e-mail.

1. Do you keep e-mails in your in-box to remind you to do something? Get a real to-do list. Your e-mail box is not a to-do list. Well, for some of you maybe it is, but it shouldn't be. Your to-do list is very important. It determines what you will get done in your life. It determines what your priorities are and what you value. So why would you let someone else dictate your to-do list?

If your in-box is your to-do list, then you have so little control over that list that you don't even add your own stuff. (Unless you are sending yourself e-mails, which is so dysfunctional that I'm not even going to make it an item in this list.) If you aren't writing the items on your to-do list, then you are not controlling your own destiny. Really, it's that serious. So write a note to yourself on your to-do list about each e-mail, prioritize it, and then delete.

2. Does it take you more than forty-eight hours to respond to people you love? This is lame. It's actually lame when responding to anyone, but especially for people you love. A forty-eight-hour response is the expectation of e-mail. If you can't meet it, don't use it. It's like this: if you respond to an IM ten hours later, you're not using IM, you're using e-mail. And if you respond six days later to an e-mail, you may as well write a letter.

If people you love send you stupid e-mails that you don't want to have to respond to, then tell the person directly. This is a much more effective way to operate than to passive-aggressively take a long time to respond.

3. Is your in-box filled with e-mails you don't want to answer? Try re-sorting. I usually sort by date sent, but when I accidentally sorted by sender, I noticed that I owed 80 percent of my responses to five people and 20 percent to 20 people. Just knowing that encouraged me to get moving. Instead of thinking of the task as thirty e-mails, I could think of it as five people. Much easier.

Here's a game I play with myself: no reading unless I'm deleting. Either I respond right away or file the e-mail and add it to my to-do list. That's a lot of work—filing and adding. So I tend to answer quickly and right away. And the more practice I get answering e-mail quickly, the easier it becomes.

I've noticed that the primary cause for my not answering an e-mail right away is not that I'm unsure of what to say; it's that I think I need to say something amazing. But e-mails need to be timely more than they need to be amazing.

Something else I noticed. It's fine to respond with a quickie one-sentence e-mail when you are getting back to someone right away. But if you wait five days to respond, and then send a quickie sentence, you look like a procrastinator.

On the other hand, if you spend all day answering your e-mail obsessively, you also scream to people that you're losing your mind. Because if you answer all mail as soon as it comes in, you're not doing your real job—unless your only job is to answer e-mail.

31. NETWORKING FOR INTROVERTS

Most people who hide behind their e-mail are doing it because they are introverts—all contact is stressful for an introvert, but face-to-face is the hardest. The thing is, if you don't get past this, you won't be able to effectively manage yourself among your coworkers.

I have a lot of empathy for people who hide behind their computers. In college I was such an introvert that when I went to parties (I had to be dragged), I brought a book. It was a lonely existence, but the pain of having to talk to people in an unstructured environment was too much.

So I was shocked a few years ago when someone told me, "Job hunting is easier for you than most people because you could sell yourself to anyone."

That comment was testament to the fact that I had recognized you can't get what you want in life without networking. Even though my natural instinct is to sit home and read, I worked very hard to learn how to talk to people. Luckily for me, books are a great resource in this regard.

I read everything I could find. I read that most introverts are scared they'll say something stupid or have nothing to say at all (both applied to me). I read up on ways to feel self-confident in a room full of strangers and come up with things to say when I felt intimidated. (Here's a recommendation: *You Are the Message,* by Roger Ailes.)

I learned that people who are good at networking are interested in other people. And they are good storytellers. After that, I was able to go almost anywhere and talk with people. Good talkers recognize that there's something interesting about every person and it's their job to get them talking about it. But you can't only bombard people with questions. You also need to reveal things about yourself. The best way is by telling fun and interesting stories that make you look good.

Not everyone can do this, though. After I had been dating my husband for about six months, I watched him print out a spreadsheet of names and phone numbers. "What's this?" I asked.

"It's my networking list," he replied.

"But you never call anyone, ever."

"I know, but networking is important, and I read that the first step is to have a good list."

It was an extremely detailed list. For every name, there was a phone number and description of the person. For example, "Bennie Conover. High school music teacher—dead." And my favorite, "Penelope Trunk. Girlfriend."

But my husband is an introvert, someone who loves details but hates talking to people. If you're similarly introverted, you can still network even though you'll never get excited about going to parties and learning interesting things about each person in the room. These tips can help.

Use e-mail. You can write and rewrite your message until it's right. And you don't have to worry about saying something stupid because the person caught you off guard. Of course, you lose the intimacy of a personal meeting, but sometimes you can compensate for this by sending an extra e-mail or two.

Read everything. When something is published about someone you know, send a congratulatory e-mail. Incessant reading means getting gossip without having to gossip. Just be
sure to act on it.

Write a blog. A blogger puts herself out in the world as
someone who is interesting and engaging—just the type
of person everyone wants to meet. "A blog increases your
network because a blog is about introducing yourself and
sharing information," says branding consultant Catherine
Kaputa.

Comment on blogs. Find a blogger you want in your network and start commenting on his blog. A comment is a
way to start a conversation with a blogger. Inserting yourself into that person's online community makes you a de
facto part of his network. Comment a lot and he might
start a side conversation with you.

Go to parties rather than dinners. If you're like most introverts, the problem isn't the quantity of people, it's having to show up at all. You can kill more birds with one
stone by making one of your rare social appearances in
front of lots of people. And think ahead: have a few things
prepared and ready to say to other partygoers.

Write for trade publications. While you aren't actually
talking to people, you're reaching them, making a point,
and hopefully being memorable. A reader may even write
back to you. Miracle! You have just made a work contact
without leaving your home.

Help others. For instance, send leads to jobseekers you know. You don't have to talk to them, but they'll remember the favor and view you as a friend. My husband maintains a list of specialized job sites that he sends to friends who have recently lost jobs. They're grateful for his help and the time it saves them, while my husband is grateful that he only has to research job sites instead of having to talk to people.

Send New Year's cards. Sending cards at the end of the year is tantamount to saying, "You're someone I care about." So send cards generously. If you can, include a short note to each person. Sure, it's a struggle to find what to say, but start thinking about this in early November, so you have two months to come up with things. Write a few cards each day, and when you're stuck for words, remember the key to good networking: be interested in other people and talk about yourself in interesting ways. Networking is one of those long-range, money-in-the-bank types of things; you never know when something you say will have a great return. So introverts, start writing!

32. E-MAILS WILL BE YOUR EPITHET: FIVE YOU SHOULD NEVER SEND

How many more investment bankers need to show up in court before people stop incriminating themselves in writing? E-mail is one of the most convenient ways to be impetuously stupid, so if you are writing an e-mail you wouldn't want your boss to read—or the SEC, or your grandma—then don't send it.

Assume that everything you write via e-mail will appear in the business section of the newspaper. Compose your messages with care and pause before you send them. Ask yourself, "Does this e-mail make me look good?" Obviously, if you are about to lie or cheat, do not send an e-mail to document your lack of ethics. But there are some other, less obvious types of e-mail that won't make you a felon, but they won't make you look good either, so don't send them.

1. *The you're-a-screw-up e-mail.* If you need to tell someone they did a bad job, do it in person so you can gauge their reaction. For example, if you open with "Your negligence on this project cost the department $2 million," and then the employee starts crying, you probably shouldn't continue in an extremely angry tone—at least not until they compose themselves. Another reason not to reprimand via e-mail: people will leave this type of e-mail in their in-box for weeks and weeks and reread it every time they want to resurrect their hate for you. Talking in person helps everyone move past the conflict without sour residue.

2. The *I'm-a-screw-up* e-mail. Do not document your weaknesses. If you must apologize for botching a project, do it in person so there is no e-mail record of your mistake for people to forward around the office. The more documentation you leave, the more your mistake festers in people's minds. And for God's sake, do not send a mass e-mail to apologize. You will invariably announce your screw-up to people who would never have heard of it otherwise.

3. The *bcc* e-mail. This e-mail function is usually for people who are insecure, manipulative, and undermining of their coworkers. Even if you are this type of person, do not announce it to everyone by using the bcc function. Sure, only the people in the bcc line realize you're using it, but all those people will understand that you are not strong enough to let everyone know who's reading the e-mail. If you feel compelled to use the bcc function, ask yourself why. Then get up off your chair, go deal with the problem face-to-face, and go back to your desk to send a more honest e-mail.

4. The *joke* e-mail. Even if it's the funniest joke of all time, do not send it to your coworkers. Why make the announcement that you read spam during work hours? Do you really have such disrespect for your own time? You might think that telling a joke is a good way to establish rapport, but a spam joke is unoriginal and impersonal, and it does nothing to make you closer to coworkers who matter. Besides, if someone thinks the joke is stupid, she will think you are stupid for sending it.

5. The Dear John e-mail. I am amazed at how many people break up via e-mail from the office. I realize that some people are such dirt bags that they don't deserve a nice breakup. I also realize that if you handle a breakup from your office, then the pressures of work can distract you from the drama of your personal life. But I am certain that there will be a Web site—maybe a new section on Match.com—for people to publish breakup e-mails they receive. Your name will be mud in the dating world if you are known for sending breakup e-mails from work.

The bottom line is that sending an e-mail is like getting dressed in the morning—both are ways to manage the way people perceive you. The only difference is that if you have a terrible outfit, you can take it off and never wear it again. A terrible e-mail propagates in cyberspace and will seem, to the original sender, to live forever.

CHAPTER ELEVEN

Get What You Want From Your Boss

You need to get along very well with your boss. Not just okay—that won't get you far. You need your boss to love working with you so much that she'll go out of her way to keep you happy.

There is no point to staying in a job if you don't get along with your boss. It's stressful to spend so much time with someone you don't like. But also, a bad relationship with your boss is incredibly limiting to you both in terms of professional development and having control over your personal life.

For the most part, there are two kinds of people: those who get along with bosses and those who don't. If you understand that your job is to keep your boss happy, then you'll get along with every boss because you'll make it such a high priority. If you get sidetracked by your own needs, or things you *think* your boss should care about, then your boss probably won't like you all that much.

People who get along with their bosses do it routinely because getting along doesn't depend on whom you work for. It's all about attitude. Your attitude should be accommodating, professional, and thick-skinned (i.e., don't take things personally). Invest a lot of time in understanding your boss's personal deficits so that when they pop up you can leverage them to work in your favor rather than complain that they are holding you back. This is called managing up, and you'd better do it. Every day.

This chapter will show you how to be a person who manages up successfully, so that you are giving your boss what she needs and your boss is giving you what you need as well.

33. THERE ARE NO BAD BOSSES, ONLY WHINY EMPLOYEES

Want to deal with a bad boss? First, stop complaining. Unless your boss breaks the law, you don't have a bad boss; you have a boss you are managing poorly. Pick on your boss all you want, but if you were taking responsibility for your career, you wouldn't let your boss's problems bring you down.

Everyone has something to offer. Find that in your boss and focus on learning everything you can. Or leave. The good news is that in most cases, you don't have to leave. You just need to manage your relationship with your boss with more empathy, more distance, and more strategy.

My favorite example of managing a bad boss is one I had at a software company. My boss refused to learn how to use a computer. I conducted most communication with him via phone, and I often played the role of secretary even though I was a vice president. He once said to me, "You're such a fast typist!" And I thought, "You're such a complete idiot!"

But in truth, he was not. He was a top negotiator and dealmaker. I stepped back and recognized that he was overwhelmed with the prospect of changing the way he had been working for twenty years, and I was in a position to help him. I found that the more dependent he was on me for e-mail, the more I was able to insert myself into high-level deals that he would not otherwise have let me in on. I helped him avoid having to change, and he taught me how to be a dealmaker.

It's always important to weigh the benefits. A good boss would have learned to type and never would have thought of delegating his typing to a vice president. But I didn't have a good boss. I had a typical boss—one with poor execution of good intentions. He had knowledge and skills to offer me as long as I could manage our relationship productively. I never expected him to manage the relationship for us, because I wanted to make sure I was getting what I needed out of it.

I could have spent my time complaining. There was a lot to complain about. Instead, I always approached him with empathy and knew when to put my two cents in and when to shut up.

Aside from cutting a deal, he didn't have a lot of management skills, and this gap left more room for me to shine. My solid interpersonal skills helped fill in what he was missing and helped me get what I wanted: a (reluctant and difficult but ultimately) very useful mentor.

So take another look at the boss you call bad. Think about what motivates him: What is he scared about that you can make easier? What is he lacking that you can compensate for? What does he wish you would do that you don't? Once you start managing this relationship more skillfully, you will be able to get more from your boss in terms of coaching and support. You will be able to tip the scales from the bad boss side to the learning opportunity side.

In fact, you should always hope for a little incompetence on your boss's part. The hole in his list of talents provides a place for you to shine. That's the point, after all, and no one shines when they're complaining.

34. BE CURIOUS AND SAY NO

You could save your company $10 million but if your boss doesn't know, it's like it never happened. So you need to systematically make sure your boss perceives that you are doing great work.

Recognition for your achievements is essential to getting what you want from work. When you ask for anything from your boss—a raise, a flexible workweek, or a better project, for example—you are really asking for your boss to acknowledge your achievements and reward you accordingly.

Here are seven ways to make sure your boss thinks you're doing a great job:

1. Know your boss's priorities. If your boss is a numbers person, quantify all your results. And know which numbers matter most to him—all numbers people have their pet line items. If your boss is a customer-is-first kind of guy, frame all your results in terms of benefits to customers. Let's say, though, that you are working on a project that is impossible to frame in terms of the customer. Then the project probably isn't a high priority for your boss, so it shouldn't be a high priority for you.

2. Say no. Say yes to the things that matter most to your boss. Say no to most everything else, and your boss will appreciate that you are focused on her needs. Remember that your boss doesn't always know everything you've got on your plate. So when she asks you to do something that you don't have time to do, ask your boss about her priorities. Let her know that you want to make sure you finish what is most important, and this will probably mean saying no to the lesser projects.

3. Communicate the way your boss does. If your boss likes e-mail, use it. If your boss prefers voice mail, phone in your updates. Convey information to your boss in the way she likes so that she's more likely to retain it. Be aware of detail thresholds, too—some people like a lot and some people like none. A good way to figure out what your boss wants is to watch how she communicates with you—she's probably doing it the way she likes best.

4. Toot your own horn. Each time you do something that impacts the company let your boss know. Leave a voice mail announcing that a project went through. Send a congratulation e-mail to your team and copy your boss. This not only draws attention to your success but also to your leadership skills. Whatever the mechanism, you need to let your boss know each time you achieve something that matters to her.

5. Lunch with your boss. If all things are equal, your boss will promote the person she likes the best. So go out to lunch and talk about what interests her. Get her on your side by asking her for advice on something about work. If you are very different than your boss, work hard to find common ground in your conversations—everyone has common ground if you hunt hard enough.

6. Seek new responsibilities. Find important holes in your department before your boss notices them. Take responsibility for filling those holes and your boss will appreciate not only your foresight, but also your ability to do more than your job. (The trick, of course, is to make sure you do not shirk your official job duties while taking on more.)

7. Be curious. Remember to make time to read and listen. Then ask questions when they are not expected; you will make yourself more interesting to be around, and you will elicit fresh ideas from everyone around you. Your boss will feel like having you on the team improves everyone's work—even his own—and that, after all, is your primary job in managing up.

The conversations in which you ask your boss for something are important to your career—those are the moments when you get what you want and you steer your path. Managing up is the groundwork you do before you start one of these important conversations. So, in effect, each day you focus on the details of managing up, you are taking care of the big-picture goals you have for your work and your life.

35. HOW TO MANAGE A BOOMER BOSS

Here's one of the hottest topics in management training: how to manage the current crop of twentysomethings. Really. Baby boomers are sitting in seminars for hours and hours trying to demystify the alien ways of the new workforce.

But what about the opposite situation? One of the most classic pieces of career advice is to manage up: manage what your boss thinks of you; steer your boss's plans for you; get your boss to supervise in a way that works well for you. Younger workers need to know how to manage their baby boomer bosses.

Managing up will not be easy. You're dealing with someone so different from you that he sits through PowerPoint presentations about emoticons. But there's hope for you, because managing up has always been a generational challenge. "All generations are angered that the next generation is not like them," says Lynne Lancaster, coauthor of *When Generations Collide: Who They Are. Why They Clash. How to Solve the Generational Puzzle at Work.*

Once you've established that you can reliably meet your boss's weekly and monthly goals, you can let your boss know about *your* goals. To a boomer, meaningful goals might be a reserved parking space and a new title, reports Laura Shelton, coauthor of *The NeXt Revolution: What Gen X Women Want at Work and How Their Boomer Bosses Can Help Them Get It.* You need to make sure your boss understands that you want shorter-term goals and that you care most about issues like being challenged, learning new skills, and preserving your personal life.

Make your priorities clear to your boss so you don't get sidetracked in areas that are irrelevant to you. Understand what you can get from your boss so you can make reasonable, actionable requests for mentoring. When a baby boomer says, "Do you realize how many years of experience I have?" the baby boomer means, "Do you realize how long I've paid my dues? Why do you think you're entitled to challenging, interesting work immediately?"

Don't be put off by this exchange. Instead, recognize what those years of experience mean for you right now. A lot of experience doesn't mean someone is clever, likeable, or talented. But when you are dealing with people who have worked many, many years, "you can assume they have learned to deal with many different situations," says Fran Pomerantz, executive recruiter at Korn/Ferry International.

So use your boss to help you with project management and prioritization because this person has seen it all before. Your seasoned boss can identify deals that are going to blow up, policies that will derail you, and perks waiting to be claimed.

Investigate which other skills your boss has picked up over the course of his long career. Make a list of skills and knowledge you want to accumulate in the next two years. Bring the list to your boss and ask him which ones he can help you with. Then ask what sort of projects or teams can help you acquire the skills out of your boss's reach.

You're going to get the best results from your boss if you use your boss's language: the language of diplomacy, according to Dianne Durkin, president of Loyalty Factor, a company that helps older workers effectively mentor younger workers. You might want to say, "Stop talking to me about my career at this company. I'm leaving in two years to start my own." But you will get a better response if you say, "It would be a big help to me if we could focus on what I'm doing this quarter."

The other language barrier you have with your boss is IM. It's like a poorly spoken second language to boomers, if they know how to use it at all. So effective management of your boss means using e-mail. And take the time to type full words and use a spell-checker—two small concessions to get what you want from your manager.

If you do all this and you don't get what you want, you should leave. "Don't sit in a job with a baby boomer boss who doesn't get it. Vote with your feet," advises Shelton. "It costs companies so much to replace a worker that they will eventually change. And this will be a better workplace for all generations."

In the end, managing a boomer boss is like managing your relationship with anyone: learn their expectations of the relationship and meet as many as you can so that you get your expectations met as well.

CHAPTER TWELVE

Don't Be the
Hardest Worker

Don't be the hardest worker. You shouldn't look lazy, but if you work the most hours you typically look the most desperate. After all, why do you need to work so much harder than the next person? Are you not as smart? Not as organized? Not as confident in your ability to navigate a non-work world? In many cases all three are true for those who work the hardest.

The fact that the hardest worker is not necessarily the most successful rears its head before a person even enters the workforce. A study conducted by Alan Krueger, professor of economics at Princeton University, shows that when it comes to workplace success, it doesn't matter if you get into an Ivy League school, it matters if you apply. Those who applied and those who got in had the same amount of success beyond those who did not apply. In this case, what matters is ambition and self-image, not getting the best grades or having the best test scores.

Nonstop work offers diminishing returns after graduation as well. People who work longer than the typical eight-hour day start to lose their effectiveness quickly. "If you work all the time, you lose your edge," warns Diane Fassel, CEO of the workplace survey firm Newmeasures and author of *Working Ourselves to Death: The High Cost of Workaholism and the Rewards of Recovery.* "Often these people are perfectionists, controlling and not good team players." The hardest workers are "not the best producers in terms of efficiency and creativity." So don't tell yourself that you work nonstop because you love your work: if you really loved your work, you'd take a break so you don't mess it up.

Ironically moments that elevate your level of success at work often require time away from work. For example, a grand idea that impacts your company's bottom line probably won't come to you when your brain is entrenched in workplace minutiae. Anyone can work the hardest, but only special people can sit back and come up with a brilliant idea. This often requires taking a break from work. In fact, even daily troubleshooting requires some mental space. The most effective workers often need to take a step back from their work to see clearly what the problem is and what the solution is.

If you can't stop working, you might be in for a negative result: workaholism. Kevin Kulic, professor of psychology at Mercy College, says, "With any of those 'holics,' you are one if it causes you or other people a problem."

But some people purposely create imbalance. "For many people, workaholism is about perfectionism or avoidance," says Kulic. The hardest workers have actually lost the self-confidence to stop working. They are either terrified of making a mistake or a misstep, or they are terrified of the world that lies beyond their work—for example, crumbling personal relationships.

Kulic cites the Yerkes-Dodson law that says too much or too little stimulation is bad. We need a happy medium in order to perform best. And Fassel cites worker surveys that support this law—the happiest workers have a workload that falls in between very heavy and very light.

Giving yourself time to think does not come naturally in the work environment. You need to train yourself. This chapter tells you how to get off the treadmill and how to rearrange your life so that you can be effective—and have time and energy left for what really matters to you.

36. DIFFERENTIATE YOURSELF BY STARING AT THE WALL

Here are some grand thoughts I bet you wish you'd had: viral marketing, routers, $E=mc^2$. We all want to have grand ideas. And if they cannot be grand enough to change the world, we at least want to make a little impact at the office.

When was the last time you had a grand epiphany in an important meeting? Probably never. The more important the meeting, the more important it is to think before you go. And the more important the audience, the more tense you are, and the more unlikely it is that you will think of something grand.

Grand thinking requires space, flexibility, and time. These are things that are hard to find if you have a life in which you balance a job with carpools or bar hopping or long trips to large families. These are also hard things to find if you never leave the office. Grand thinking requires time alone doing nothing, or almost nothing. Eve Bunting, an award-winning children's book author, once said she got most of her book ideas while she was swimming laps. One of my favorite bosses told me that the reason he took a shower every morning was not to be clean, but to have time to think.

The problem with most people's schedules is that they work hard to get ahead, but the real way people get ahead is by having good ideas. You can file and file and always be trying to catch up on filing, or you can stop, rest, and think of a new filing system that will keep you from falling behind. You're probably not a secretary, and you probably don't file, but you probably have the equivalent problem that is running you ragged.

Take advantage of a slow time at work to make a new routine. You need a routine for thinking. And remember, it doesn't take ten minutes. It takes ten minutes just to stop thinking about all the stuff you could be doing at work instead of thinking. You are going to have to schedule time and make a commitment to keeping it. Thinking time is not "Any time my boss cancels a meeting with me, I'll use the time to think." Thinking time is not "Some time on Saturday," because if you do not have a set time, it will never happen. You can find thinking time in your electronic calendar by leveraging the "repeat date" function. You can find thinking time on your wall calendar by marking it in red felt tip so you can't miss it and can't erase it.

I do my best thinking on the treadmill. When I first started running on the treadmill instead of outside, I was shocked to see people reading while they ran—you'd never see that in a park. I wondered when these people emptied their brains if they were using the best brain-emptying time by filling them. I also do good thinking on the subway. When I first moved from Los Angeles to New York I felt car withdrawal. I missed my stereo. I missed my leather seats. Now I realize that the mindlessness of riding the subway is a gift for good thinking. I stare into space. I relax for the ride. I wait for an idea to hit me. Not that this happens every day, but a big step toward having a good idea is being available with a clear mind so that an idea has a place to appear.

Stop and think. And get used to the feeling; it's good. In addition to that, it's super-productive, because the big ideas are what get you noticed at work. Small ideas influence small portions of work—probably your own. Big ideas influence teams and whole companies. If you want your boss and coworkers to treat you like a person with ideas that matter, then you need to have some.

37. A LONG LIST OF WAYS TO DODGE LONG HOURS

It's hard to leave the office at a reasonable time of day when your workplace culture centers on long hours. But the cost of not leaving work is high: a half-built life and career burnout.

Of course, if you never work long hours, you will never appear committed enough to get to the top ranks. So your job is to work enough hours to look committed but not so many hours that you risk your personal life and your ability to succeed over the long haul. People cannot work full-speed until they die. Pace yourself so you don't burn out before you reach your potential.

But don't blame your long hours on your boss, your CEO, or your underlings. If you don't make a conscious, organized effort to take responsibility for the number of hours you work, you can be thrown off course by anyone. But if you systematically follow the steps below, you will not be thrown off course, even by a workaholic boss in a workaholic industry:

Concentrate on quality of work over quantity. The person who builds a career on doing the most work commits to living on a treadmill. The work will never be done and you will become known among your coworkers as someone who never turns down an assignment. Read: dumping ground. Quality is what matters. People don't lose a job for not working unpaid overtime; they lose a job for not performing well at the most important times. A resume is not a list of hours worked, it is a list of big accomplishments.

Know the goals of your job. You need to know the equivalent of a home run in your job. Get a list of goals from your boss and understand how they fit into the big picture. Judge if your work is high quality by what people need from you and how they measure success. Be sure to get goals that are quality-oriented and not hours-oriented. Suggest replacing "Devote eight hours a week to cold-calling" to "Find six qualified leads in three months."

Find the back door. Figure out what criteria people use for promotion. It is never only how many hours you work. In many professions you need to work a lot of hours, but there is always a way to be impressive enough to cut back on hours. In the realm of superstars, achievement is based on quality over quantity. Figure out how to turn out extremely impressive work so that you can get away with fewer hours. For example, if you're a lawyer, you could pick up one very important client for the firm and then cut back a little on your hours.

Refuse bad assignments. Figure out what matters and spend your time on that. Once you have clear short-term and long-term goals, it's easy to spot the person you don't need to impress, the project that will never hit your resume, or the hours worked that no one will notice.

Say no. Constantly. The best way to say no is to tell people what is most important on your plate so they see that, for you, they are a low priority. Prioritizing is a way to help your company, your boss, and yourself. No one can fault you for that.

Go public. Tell people about your schedule ahead of time. For example, "I have Portuguese lessons on Thursdays at 7 p.m. The class is important to me." When you plan a vacation, announce it early and talk about it a lot. The more people know about how much you have been preparing and anticipating your trip, the less likely they will be to ask you to cancel it.

Find a silent mentor. Look for someone who is respected but does not work insane hours. This will take careful hunting because this person is not likely to be obvious about it. Watch him from afar and figure out how he operates. Few people will want to mentor you in the art of dodging work—it's bad for a person's image. But you could enlist the person to help you in other areas and hope he decides to help you in the workload area as well.

Know your boss's goals. Your best tool for saying no to a project is reminding your boss what her goals are. If she cannot keep track of her own goals, help her. If you worm your way out of work that doesn't matter to her so that you can do work that does matter to her, she is more likely to back you up. Also, your boss will protect you from assignments from other people if you show her how other people's work affects your boss's goals.

Take control of what you can. Even small efforts at control add up to a lot, and best of all, they usually go unnoticed by others. For example, refuse to make meetings on Monday and you are less likely to have to prepare for them on the weekend. Refuse meetings after 4:30 p.m. and you are less likely to miss dinner at home. Ignore your phone while you write your weekly report and you're less likely to stay late to finish it. You don't need to tell people, "My policy is no meetings at x time." Just say you're already booked and suggest another time. You can't do this for every meeting, but you can do it enough to make a difference in your life.

Know your own boundaries. Wanting to work fewer hours is too vague a goal because you won't know which hours to protect. Try getting home by 7 p.m., not working weekends, or leaving for two hours in the middle of the day to lift weights. These are concrete goals for cutting back hours.

Create something important outside of work. If you don't create a life outside of work that is joyful and engaging, then you won't feel a huge need to leave work. And if you don't project a passion for life outside of work, then no one will think twice about asking you to live at work.

So get some passion in your personal life. If you can't think of anything, start trying stuff: snowboarding, pottery, speed dating. The only way to discover new aspects of yourself is to give them new opportunities to come out.

Be brave. Brave people can say no when someone is pushing hard, and brave people can go home when other people are working late. The bravery comes from trusting yourself to find the most important work and to do it better than anyone else.

But sometimes the bravest thing to do is leave. Some jobs—for example, coding video games, or being a low-level analyst at an investment bank—are so entrenched in the idea that workers have no lives that you will find yourself battling constantly to get respect for your personal life. In some cases, you are better off changing industries, or at least changing companies.

38. A MESSY DESK MAKES YOU LOOK INCOMPETENT

Here's a scenario that happens all the time. There's a messy desk next to a clean desk, and someone says to the guy with the messy desk, "Can you please clean up your desk? Look at the one next to you! Yours is a mess." The messy-desker says, "His desk is clean because he gets nothing done." The messy-desker is wrong.

Not wrong about who is getting more done. Maybe the messy desk is a sign that the person has double the workload of the person with the clean desk. It doesn't matter. You have to have a clean desk to project an organized image. So do less work and clean up your desk.

Don't tell yourself things like, "My work gets done. I know where everything is. People are too concerned about appearances." All these things could be true. But here is what is also true: if your desk is a mess, you look overwhelmed and less competent. This isn't about what is happening in your head, it is about what is happening in your coworkers' heads, and they are judging you by the appearance of your desk.

The FBI has known for decades that you can judge people by their workspace, which is why it has special investigators who visit the offices of criminals. The FBI doesn't publish its data on this type of investigation, but the University of Texas does. And a study conducted there found that people with messy offices are perceived as less efficient, less organized, and less imaginative than people with clean desks.

People judge a mess. "There is a cultural bias toward orderliness," says Eric Abrahamson, professor at Columbia Business School. Kelly Crescenti, an Illinois-based career coach, concurs: "When people have a clean desk, it looks like they get things done and they are productive." If you have a messy desk, even if you get every project done well, the perception will be that you don't.

Some of you who are stubborn (and delusional) are saying, "So what? That's not me." But even if you are definitely sure that you are as efficient in your messy office as your neighbor is in her clean office, your coworkers don't see it that way. It's true that some people are efficient with their messy desk, according to Julie Morgenstern, organizing guru and author of *Never Check E-mail in the Morning: And Other Unexpected Strategies for Making Your Work Life Work*. But she concedes that "the image issue is giant."

You have to manage your image because it matters more than what you say. When you talk, for the most part, people do not listen: they look. Sixty to ninety percent of conversation is interpreted through nonverbal communication, according to Anne Warfield of Impression Management Professionals. A messy desk falls into the image management category, and the messiness undermines your career in subtle ways. If you are the owner of the company, you give the impression that you cannot handle your position and the company is in trouble. If you are in middle management, when someone is giving away a plum assignment, she does not think of you because you give the impression that it will go into a pile and never come out. Even the person at the bottom rung of a company has to

look organized. If your boss sends you to the copy machine
for an eternity, the only way to show you deserve more
responsibility is to look like you can handle it: all those
papers to copy and all those collated piles must be very
orderly on your desk.

Still not convinced? Would you ever go to work in
purple-and-green-striped pants and a Hawaiian shirt? Why
not? You could still do your job. But people would not perceive that you could still do your job because appearances
are powerful, and someone who dresses in a goofy, unconventional way does not inspire confidence. Appearances
matter, and the desk in your office is as important as the
clothes on your back.

But when it comes to projecting a positive image
through your personal space, some areas are more easily
managed than others, and a messy desk is tough. If you
keep a messy desk you may have to fundamentally change
your behavior in order to clean up your act.

Start a filing system. Each piece of paper you get should
either go in the garbage or into a file. Don't let it sit on your
desk for more than three hours. This means every three
hours you have to attend to your filing system.

Another key to organizing is to keep a good to-do list.
The list should be prioritized as A, B, and C tasks. You
won't need to keep stuff on your desk to remind you to do
A, B, and C before you go home because your to-do list
will tell you.

As with all image management advice, don't go over-
board. Abrahamson provides a postmodern defense of the
messy desk: "Messiness is related to creativity because it
tends to juxtapose things that don't normally go together,"

he says. And, he reports that he has seen computer desktops that rival the worst of the classic desktop messes. "It's the last frontier of messiness," he says. So while it's true that your coworkers can accurately judge you by looking at your workspace, it's also true that your computer desktop is a nice place to hide your worst attributes, if you must.

The issue here is not if you are productive as a worker. The issue is whether you are productive as an image manager, because if you are not managing your image at work, you are not managing your career. Use your workspace to control how people perceive you. A side benefit to this project will be that you might actually become a little more productive once that filing system is in place.

CHAPTER THIRTEEN

Getting a Promotion Is So Last Century

Can we all just stop talking about promotions like they matter? A promotion has meaning when someone is moving up the corporate ladder at such a slow pace that every small step is grounds for celebration.

But there are no longer corporate ladders because no one stays long enough at a company to get up the whole ladder. And even if someone did try to climb, he'd probably be laid-off, outsourced, or off-shored before getting to the top. Instead of focusing so much on getting a promotion, turn your focus on what you really want and need right now: interesting work and a chance to expand your skill set.

So what is the point of a promotion? *More* responsibility, which implicitly comes with a promotion, is not what you want. You want the *right kind* of responsibility—which means work you can learn from and increase your marketability with. A raise is, of course, nice. But when you really think about it, a typical raise is hardly something to get excited about.

Here is a headline from Salary.com: "Raise Outlook Better Than Employees Expected." The article goes on to say that the average raise was something just above 3 percent. Let's say 4 percent. This means if you were making $50,000 a year, you'd get $2,000 a year more. *So what?* Does that change your life? In fact, if you adjust for the increase in cost of living, it's more like $1,000, and if you take out taxes, you are looking at a little more than $700 a year. What's that going to buy you? Pretty much nothing. It will not change your life in any significant way, that's for sure.

The next time you think a promotion is what you want, think again. Ask your boss for what really matters, and if a promotion follows as a result, so be it, but don't ask for a promotion per se. Ask for items like these:

1. Growth opportunities. Learning new skills is worth a lot more to you, in the long run, than some ridiculous 4 percent raise. Ask to get on a team that will teach you how to do something you think is important. Ask to work with the clients who are doing the most innovative projects. Get on a project with the person in the company you admire most so you can understand how she operates.

Or look for off-site resources. Request a training budget and send yourself to a bunch of seminars. You can read all you want, but the best way to really learn something is to role-play, which everyone hates to do, so go to a seminar where someone forces you to do it.

2. Mentor opportunities. Ask to be matched with a mentor in the company. This is not a revolutionary request. Human resource executives have been studying this process for more than a decade and they know how to pick someone good for you. They just need to spend a little time doing it.

Also ask to sit in on meetings you wouldn't normally get to see. If you're an engineer, sit in on a marketing meeting, for example. You'll find out more about how businesses operate and how people think, and you might even stumble on something you really like. If you are in management, ask to sit in on a very high-level meeting so you can better understand the decision-making process at the top.

3. Flex-time opportunities. If your company values you as an employee, perhaps instead of asking for a promotion you could suggest that you keep your current job but do it from home or do it four days a week. After all, you've already shown you perform well. Heck, ask to work from Tahiti; you may be able to do the job however and wherever you want as long as you maintain your stellar level of performance.

4. Entrepreneurial opportunities. Just say no. To the promotion, that is. Now that you have a sense of how much time and energy your current job requires, and now that you've mastered the scope, you can try something on the side. Use your extra time to start your own business. The safest way to experiment with running your own business is to do it while you still have a regular paycheck. Who cares if it doesn't include that 4 percent raise? Think of your paycheck as a research grant for your ideas for a side business.

Instead of letting last century's carrots dictate your workplace rewards, think about what is right for you, right now. What do you really need? You don't need a promotion. It's something else. Think about what would really make a difference in your life and then make it happen. While the rest of your organization is focusing on titles and money, you can slip under the radar and get something truly meaningful.

This chapter will give you other ways to think about a promotion. The fact is, besides offering very little, promotions do not come quickly or easily. So this chapter will also give you ways to get what you need from a company without holding out hope for an incredible promotion, or a boss who looks out for your very best interests. Here are some ideas for taking your career into your own hands.

39. YOU ONLY NEED $40,000 A YEAR TO BE HAPPY

Looking for happiness through financial success? Wondering what the magic number is? It's $40,000. Really. So pick a job you are going to enjoy instead of one that makes a lot of money—just be sure your job will get you to that $40,000 mark. And if you're still not happy when you're making that much money, the problem is not that you can't buy things. The problem is something else.

The problem with money is that no matter how much we have, we think we need more. Our instincts developed in the conditions when we were hunter-gatherers. Today we are genetically predisposed to want more of whatever we are collecting, even though there is plenty, according to Terry Burnham, an economics professor at Harvard's Kennedy School of Government, and Jay Phelan, a professor of biology at UCLA. (For a good read—and primal justification for obsessively eating the candy in your desk drawer—check out their book *Mean Genes: From Sex to Money to Food; Taming Our Primal Instincts*.)

I remember when I passed the $100,000 mark. My boss loved my work and gave me a raise that put me at $125,000. Soon a competitor offered me $140,000 and my boss told me he wouldn't match it. At that point I had no kids, no mortgage, and no car payments, so I didn't need the money. But I recognized salary as a gauge of prominence in my field, and although I was making $125,000, I felt underappreciated. So I took the $140K.

Eventually, I left that job for one that paid more than $200,000 a year, and I lived the aphorism that you have to spend money to make money. I couldn't take high-end clients out to dinner in my refurbished wreck of a car, so I leased a BMW. I had to dress as well as my clients, so I bought designer suits. And since my new position left no time to manage my personal life, I hired an assistant to manage it.

You might scoff at my choices, but I was not unique among those whose salaries hit six figures: my expenses rose with my salary, and my desires expanded with my bank account. You might think, "That won't happen to me," but think twice before assuming you would be the exception to the rule.

In fact, this salary guideline is well established in research: the first $40,000 makes a big difference in a person's level of happiness. Happiness is dependent on being able to meet basic needs for food, shelter, and clothing. After meeting those needs you have to turn to something other than consumerism, because additional money has negligible impact on how happy you are. Your level of happiness is instead largely dependent on your outlook.

I have found this to be true. When my husband and I both made career changes, we lived on less than $40,000 in New York City for more than a year. With a small child. That was a very bad time. When I tell people you only need $40,000 to be happy, most people's response is, "In which city?" or, "With how many kids?" But when you are dealing with less than $40,000, the city and the number of kids become less important. For example, there is no going out to dinner, so there is no extra bill for an extra kid. There is just a box of pasta, which is only about fifty cents more if you add another person. In any city.

When we began making just over $40,000 a year, the tides turned dramatically because we didn't have to worry about any necessities. Just like the research says: you can't worry about dealing with your happiness if you are dealing with necessities. So stop fixating on if $40,000 is the real number. It is. People who refuse to believe that $40,000 is all you need to be happy are people who do not want to take responsibly for fixing the things in their lives that have nothing to do with money.

Maybe you're thinking there's another magic threshold beyond $40,000. Like maybe $40 million. But you're wrong. When I ran in the circles of venture capitalists, there was a common phrase, "It's not jet money." This was a way of saying, it was a good deal, but it won't earn enough money to buy and maintain a private jet. No matter what size the pile of money is, there's always a way to see it as small.

What you need to do is change your outlook. About money, about work. That's what will make the big difference.

40. CIRCUMVENT HIERARCHY BY JOINING A TEAM

One of the defining traits of Generation Y is its penchant, and talent, for working in teams. Enzo Marchio, Antonio DeFabritiis, and Johnny Marchio are equal owners of the hair salon Enzo & Company, and they are a good example of this team mentality. Unlike entrepreneurs of the past, who were typically loners who were uncomfortable functioning in a larger organization, these three would never think of going it alone. DeFabritiis says, "Everything is easier if we work as a team. And it's more fun." When asked how he learned to work well in a team, DeFabritiis says, "This is how we were brought up."

Bruce Tulgan, founder of RainmakerThinking and coauthor of *Managing Generation Y,* explains that there was a big shift in parenting, teaching, and counseling in the mid-80s because of research in childhood self-esteem. "These kids are very well-versed in getting along with others, collaboration skills, feeling part of a team, and having good communication skills."

Teams appeal to young workers because they have no interest in boring or ancillary workplace tasks, even at the entry level. Well-constructed teams provide an opportunity to be a decision maker and a key contributor early in your career. According to Tulgan, "Generation Yers like teams because they are pulled out of the hierarchical structure. On a team it's not about what is your experience, but what can you do today."

Being part of a team is the best way for today's new

workers to get interesting high-level work for themselves. However, even though reams of research shows the effectiveness of teams in the workplace, baby boomer management has had a tough time with implementation.

Older, more experienced workers are more comfortable in hierarchies, especially since they are the workers most likely to be on top. Often, according to Tulgan, the idea of a corporate team is meaningless: "People just change the sign on the door from human resources department to human resources team." And, if boomers do form teams, they are often hierarchical teams in which there is one leader who tells everyone else what to do.

Jeff Snipes, CEO of Ninth House, a provider of online education, including optimizing team effectiveness, says a hierarchical, leader-oriented team was appropriate for earlier generations: "Traditionally if you worked up the ranks for twenty years and all the employees were local, then you could know all the functions of the workplace. You could lead by barking orders. But today everything moves too fast and the breadth of competency necessary to do something is too vast."

The most effective teams today are competency-based teams, in which each person comes to the group with a different skill and they work together for a specific duration on a specific project to build something bigger than themselves. On these teams, everyone is an important decision maker and is able to make a big contribution.

Workers who want to have the growth opportunities that come with competency-based teams should make sure they are choosing to work at companies that use this sort of team. Snipes suggests that you ask the following questions of a company you're considering. (Note to managers: ask yourself how you'd answers these questions. You need good answers if you're going to attract the good catches in the coming years.)

1. What sort of talent development does the company provide? There are no good teams without team training. A company committed to team leadership trains people to do it.

2. Is diversity important to the company? When it comes to teams, diverse input leads to more effective outcomes. Diversity is important not only in terms of race and culture, but also in terms of the way people think.

3. Is there a reward system in place for teams? If a company rewards only individual achievements, then individuals will have less incentive to make teams work.

But let's be real. Not everyone can stomach working on a team. Kerry Sulkowicz, founder of the Boswell Group and adviser to CEOs on psychological aspects of management, says, "There are different types of personalities and it's not as simple as being part of a generation. There will always be some people who feel constrained being part of a group." Sulkowicz says to think of it as a spectrum: almost everyone needs alone time, but some people need very little and some people need a lot. For those of you who don't do your best work in teams, take solace in the fact that baby boomers still run the workplace and they're not big on teams, either.

41. TITLE *SCHMITLE,* YOU CAN LEAD WITHOUT ONE

Leading without a title is among the most high-risk moves you can do at work. The upside is huge because it's an opportunity to show people you can lead beyond the scope of your current job, which is the best advertising you can do to get more exciting work. The downside is not only do you risk failing at something you really had no authority to do in the first place, but also that failure could ripple into the job you were actually hired to do, so you look like an all-round failure.

Still, you should do it. Always keep your eyes open for new roles that will help you gain the skills and experience you need to get you where you want to go. But use the following list to identify opportunities and make them successful—this will mitigate the downside risk to taking on a leadership role without the title.

1. Find an empty space that needs a leader. The best way to find a spot to expand your domain is to identify a problem that no one wants to take responsibility for solving.

You should only accept undocumented leadership for a project that has a beginning and an end. Otherwise, how will you show you completed the project successfully? If there is no natural beginning and end, create one before you undertake your new leadership position.

Keep in mind that if there is a true problem, there will be a true end because the problem will be solved. If there is no problem, then there is no need for you to jump in. Things are going fine.

The litmus test is when you bring the problem to the person who, technically, should be solving it. If that person says, "Oh yeah. I know about that. I'm on it," then back off. If the person says, "Oh, no. I was worried that might come up. What a mess," then come back the next day with a suggestion that you take on the problem. Do it casually, as though you have extra time and that person doesn't and you're happy to help.

2. Make a subtle transition to leader. Don't make this project about you (until the end). To make your leadership project a success, you need to downplay the fact that someone has given up on a problem and handed it to you. Do not make this person look bad since he is the key to your expanding your domain. Also, downplay the fact that you are asking a bunch of people to follow you even though they don't report to you. Everything should be casual, as if your helping out is natural. It should not appear that you are saving the day and everyone had better listen to you or else.

3. Build a team. Since you are not officially a leader, you don't have an official team. There are two ways you can build a team: by handpicking all the A-players or by working with one of the low-performing groups and making it perform beyond expectations. You have more room for accolades by doing the latter, but you also set yourself up for more risk.

In either case, you need to convince these people that the project you need help with is great for them. You cannot do this by dishing out BS. You have to really find out what these people want for themselves, and you have to be able to provide it. Most people just want to do interesting things at work through which they can learn a lot and surpass their own expectations of themselves. Craft your project in ways that afford everyone this opportunity. You may need to expand your goals, or replace a high-level person with someone who will be more excited about the opportunity. But once you get a group convinced that the project can help them meet their goals, these people will follow you to get what they want. This is a dependable kind of team, even if you have no official title.

4. Make a presentation. This is everything you are working toward. When you solve the problem you have set out to solve, create a final report to let everyone know about it. The report should be an achievement document not only for you—to let people know how well you performed in a broader leadership role—but also for the team that got you here, because each person involved has personal goals that you need to recognize in this report. The report should clearly state the problem and the quantified solution: saved money, saved time, increased sales, averted financial loss, and so forth. The report should also make recommendations for changes going forward, with quantified estimates of savings, growth, sales, etc. The implication will be that you are the one to lead these changes. But you will not say this outright. The report will speak for itself.

42. THE NEW WORKPLACE CURRENCY IS TRAINING

Title is not important if you're not staying long term. And salary increases of 3 or 4 percent are ceremonial. So use the clout you earn to get training; it will make a difference in your life in a way that salary and title cannot because training can fundamentally change how you operate and what you have to offer.

The two most important types of training teach you how to understand yourself and how you function in an office. To a large extent, you have to take responsibility for training yourself in these areas. You can't learn this stuff passively, like learning key dates in U.S. history.

"This must be a self-motivated kind of learning," says Julie Jansen, career coach and author of *You Want Me to Work with Who? Eleven Keys to a Stress Free, Satisfying, and Successful Work Life . . . No Matter Who You Work With.* "The problem is that most people don't know how self-aware they are." Jansen's book offers self-diagnostic tests to show you where you fall on the spectrum of self-awareness and how to retrain yourself.

Most people think they make a good impression, but they are misguided. A great help in gauging this is an objective third party who can tell you where you are weak—after all, everyone has weaknesses. The trick is to identify and fix them early in your working life so they don't hold you back.

Workplace stars receive great training perks. "Most companies quickly segment out high-potential employees and they get more advanced and aggressive training," says Jeff Snipes, CEO of Ninth House. "Companies don't usually market these programs because they create an atmosphere of haves and have-nots. However you can ask around at your company if there's a high-potential program and what you'd need to do to get in."

Here are some of the types of training to ask for:

1. Self-awareness coaching. Few people can accurately judge the impression they make on others. This is so widely accepted that companies are willing to pay big bucks for the 360-degree performance review, which includes in-depth interviews between a third party and a wide range of people you work with. Once you determine your weaknesses, hiring a coach is a great way to understand the results of the review and figure out how to either get rid of your weaknesses or at least get around them.

2. Communications coaching. One of the most difficult pieces of managing yourself is projecting what you really feel to other people. So many things get in the way of authenticity in the office—most notably, your ego, but also your nerves. Many companies train people to communicate by using the same techniques that an actor uses to connect with his audience. Top executives from companies you respect use this method of training all the time. If they need it, so do you. Get the training early in your career so you can make authentic connections from the beginning.

3. Training on how to navigate within a company. Many young people complain that they have great ideas but no one is listening. That's often true, but it's not enough to have innovative ideas. You need to know how to promote them within the company.

Ninth House, for example, offers training programs that teach how to package an idea so you can get it funded within the company. Topics in this program include how to align the idea with corporate strategy and how to find an internal sponsor, two critical pieces to being an innovator in the workplace.

When it comes to selling an idea at the office, don't forget that you'll have to sell the idea that training will be good for your boss as well as for you. Be sure to align the benefits of training with the needs of your company.

If you're unemployed, you can't get a company to pay, but you might ask your parents. Another way to think about training is in terms of the job hunt: many companies, such as Hayden-Wilder, teach young people how to use public relations techniques to market themselves to employers.

Whatever sort of training you use—self-generated, corporate-funded, or a mix of the two—if you create a life that encourages constant learning, your career and your life will be more interesting and more fulfilling.

CHAPTER FOURTEEN

The New American Dream Is About Time, Not Money

The American dream has changed. It used to be a college education, a steady job, a nice house (and a family to fill it), and a better financial picture than your parents. There is a new American dream that is still about "doing better than your parents" but not necessarily in a financial sense. This dream is about fulfillment.

Ariel Freiberg, a painter, just got engaged to a computer programmer, and she and her fiancé are gearing up for this new dream. "We were brought up to think it's important to own a piece of property. It's how you build your life in this country. But buying a house is not a major goal for us. It is not what will make our lives secure and it will not help us define ourselves."

"The idea of the American dream is taken out from under us," explains Anya Kamenetz, author of *Generation Debt*. "There used to be a contract with employers—health care, pensions, predicable employment," but today there are none of those guarantees.

Additionally, a college education has become so expensive that it makes it more difficult to take these first steps toward the American dream, according to Tamara Draut, author of *Strapped: Why America's 20- and 30-Somethings Can't Get Ahead.* The average student loan comes to around $20,000, which means $200 a month out of an entry-level paycheck. On top of that, between 1995 and 2002 median rents in almost all major cities increased more than 50 percent.

Hillary Clinton once gave a speech about how "a lot of kids don't know what work is" and young people "think work is a four-letter word." These were not renegade words, but rather an expression of the prevailing attitude among her fellow baby boomers.

The boomers mistake a rejection of their American dream as a rejection of reality. But here's some news: young people know that work is a reality for everyone. It's just that everyone needs to work toward something, so young people have a new American dream.

"The new American dream is much more entrepreneurial," says Kamenetz. "And it's about shaping one's own destiny: mobility, flexibility to do your own work, and the ability to have a career as an expression of who you are as a person."

The new American dream is for risk takers. This is actually not groundbreaking in terms of the American dream. For immigrants, the American dream has always meant risk-taking. But today young people are taking risks that their parents would have never dreamed of, like playing contact sports without any health insurance and signing up for a mortgage to be paid off with a freelance career.

This chapter will help you make early decisions that will be essential in crafting your own version of the new American dream. It will help you protect your time for the things that matter most and show you why you should make choices by looking inside yourself instead of getting sidetracked by the norms of the people who came before you.

Choices are difficult today because the new American dream is not as measurable as the old one. You cannot look at your bank statement or count your bedrooms to assess your success. The new American dream is about fulfillment, which is a murky, slippery goal, but you will know it when you feel it.

43. DELEGATE TO MAKE MORE TIME FOR YOURSELF

The only way to accommodate a thriving career and a thriving personal life is to cut back on what you do each time you add something to your plate. This means that as soon as the opportunity presents itself, you need to delegate work that is not intrinsically fulfilling for you.

Most managers know they should be delegating, but many still don't do it. They say they can't, and they cite instances in which they are great and their staff is not. But the truth is, managers who don't delegate would be embarrassed if they could see how they appear to others.

A boss who delegates builds trust among her staff and helps them to grow. And she allows her own growth by giving herself space. This should be motivation enough to clear everything off your plate by delegating it. If you are still having trouble delegating, here's something else that might motivate you: you look arrogant.

The most common barrier managers face when delegating is that they think they can do the work better if they do it themselves. But here's some news: all work does not need to be done the way you would do it. In fact, usually work does not need to be done perfectly to be done well. If you want to aim for perfection (which you shouldn't), try to be a perfect manager and applaud your employees who do a good job without being perfectionists.

Remember when you had your first job and someone finally let you do something beside straighten files? Well, whatever you did, believe me, you did it very poorly at first.

But someone let you try and helped you grow. So return the favor by helping someone else grow. And do not redo that person's work once it's finished. If you can't coach someone to do good work, it's your fault. You are either an incompetent coach—and you need to get better—or you are coaching someone who is incompetent, and you need to fire her.

Remember, your job is to manage the work and your employees, not to do everything yourself. A person who delegates is a person who has trust: trust in your own talent to lead, and trust in your staff's talent to perform.

So get everything off your plate today. Your staff will love you for trusting them, and you will learn a lot about yourself by facing your fear that people will not do things the way you would do them. As you become more efficient at work, you will free up more time for the important aspects of your job, and you'll have more time for your personal life.

44. MARRYING FOR MONEY IS OUT; MARRYING FOR FLEXIBILITY IS IN

For Generations X and Y, supercareers are old news. The new focus is on parenting. What used to be mistaken for a "slacker" work ethic (by a media dominated by boomer workaholics) is actually a generation-defining obsession with work-life balance. Parents expect to be closely involved with their children, and paying for full-time child care is widely rejected as inconsistent with the core values of the generation.

The workplace is not set up to accommodate these values, so you need to start very early in your career planning for your shift to parenting. Even if you don't think you want children, if you want to have a fulfilling personal life outside of work, you need to plan for it early. The careers that are flexible are well planned on many fronts—from what you study to whom you marry to where you live. Family planning is not the morning-after pill; it is the systematic development of a work-life plan executed over the course of a decade.

There are three paths for dual-career couples with children. The first path is where both partners work full-time and outsource the running of the household. This was popular when women thought they could "have it all." But women entering the workforce today know better, and most want no part of that lifestyle. For one thing, women have learned from the mistakes of the previous generations and understand the difficulties that arise with this scenario: there is no equality in taking care of kids. Even if there is a full-time nanny, one parent feels the majority of the burden on sick days, parent-teacher conferences, Halloween, and soccer games.

The second path is where one partner leaves the workforce to run the household. This path made men's careers soar for years, and it was the most popular choice when women had no choice. But it is making a comeback because many families see no other way. Among highly educated women with children, 43 percent have left their careers voluntarily during their first eight years in the workforce; this trend is on the rise. And most women at the very top of corporate America either do not have kids or have adopted this model but with a stay-at-home husband.

The third path is what Generation Xers and Yers tend to aim for: reconfigured work around the changing needs of family. This path presents an opportunity for you to be very involved in parenting on a day-to-day basis while continuing to honor your ambitions. (For a surprisingly riveting read about women and ambition, check out Anna Fels's book, *Necessary Dreams: Ambition in Women's Changing Lives.*)

However, most people are unrealistic about what the third path requires. According to Lisa Levey, director of advisory services at Catalyst, a research institute for women and business, shared care is "a tough situation to establish because the paradigm has shifted but the jobs have not."

Most career-worthy jobs are prepackaged for a forty-hour (or more) work week, which leaves little room for parents who want to be primary caretakers of their children and have economically meaningful work outside the home. According to Levey, "Five years after business school, only 60 percent of women are working outside the home. Women look ahead and the path seems impossible. You can't have two people gunning in their careers, and women are more likely to quit when there's a problem."

But when it comes to choosing that third path, Levey says sooner is better. "You have to really want it, seek it out, plan for it over a long period of time." Among the people who have successfully established a third path, they cite these steps as the most important:

1. Talk about the planning with your spouse before he or she is your spouse, and then continue the discussion because people's attitudes change all the time.

2. Understand your personal needs well so that you can make big decisions about your family's needs faster and better.

3. Prepare for big compromise. Maybe a ratty car. Maybe the house is not clean. Maybe the kids don't play soccer. No one in the family will get everything they want.

4. Negotiate with your spouse. Don't shy away from conflict. You can't get what you want if you don't bring up what you're not getting.

5. Don't compare yourself to other families. Everyone is trying something new in this area. Borrow ideas, share ideas, and keep thinking. Don't assume there's one, best way to run a family.

45. TYPECAST YOURSELF

When you plan your career, think about a specialty. Whatever you want for your personal life will come more easily if you are in high demand in your professional life. People in high demand can ask for more concessions from the workplace. Become a specialist as a way to enable yourself to develop your career even as you increase the time and energy you give to your personal life.

People think that saying they are a generalist makes them look very useful and therefore very employable. In fact, being a generalist means good at nothing and headed for long-term unemployment. Generalist is the label for a career that will die, but it's also the label for someone who is scared.

Think cars: you never hear an advertiser say, "Buy my car, it's good for everything!" Volvos are safe. BMWs are fun. Saturns are easy to buy because the dealers won't haggle. Just as successfully branded products offer specific benefits, successfully branded careerists offer specific talents. You get to the top by being the best, and you can't be the best at everything.

Ezra Zuckerman, a professor at MIT's Sloan School of Management, agrees—and he has the research to prove it. In his study of typecasting in Hollywood titled "Robust Identities or Nonentities," Zuckerman found that specialization leads to longer, more productive careers. Contrary to conventional Hollywood wisdom, big bucks come most often to people who become known for a certain type of role. Zuckerman finds that typecasting, as this practice is called, is also a moneymaker in the business world, where the hiring system is set up to reward those who differentiate themselves. "Headhunters are specialized," he says, "and they look for something they can package and sell."

Generalist is a good moniker during the first few years of your career. For example, if you're a standout college grad, you may win a place in a general-management rotational training program, such as the ones General Electric and other well-known consumer products companies offer. But the point of such training programs is to figure out what you're good at and then seek an internal role in that department.

So take a gamble. Figure out what you're best at and start making your mark. Then hope for good timing—that someone needs your particular talent when you have become an expert at it.

Linda Chernoff started out as an administrator at a law firm. She knew the job wasn't for her, so she jumped at the chance to handle alumni affairs at Temple University. Her job duties included securing football seats for big donors, calling on nondonors who were loaded, and planning tailgate parties and balls. She liked the event planning best, so she took a job doing just that at the Museum of Fine Arts in Boston. Linda's career path is one of steady, narrowing focus—she has become more and more specialized as she has figured out what she likes.

Specialization is the goal, but be wary of too much or too early. Many professionals hesitate to define themselves because it limits where they can go. But top players must have clear definition. Most have enough confidence in their abilities to risk specialization. Very simply, they believe that adequate opportunities will be available as they become more focused.

To specialize, think discipline (marketing, sales, operations, etc.) and sector (media, technology, fashion, etc.). The last step is to go very narrow to get to the very top of your field. For example, Vera Wang does wedding dresses. She is, by some standards, the best. On a more grassroots level, Anastasia Goodstein writes one of the top blogs about Generation Y trends. She started out in journalism, then focused on online media, and then began blogging about a specific age group. Like Wang and Goodstein, you need to become known for your extreme interests and talents. If you aren't extremely good at something, you won't rise above the average middle.

Still not convinced of the benefits of typecasting? Hundreds of resumes stream in for most job openings. Hiring managers and recruiters electronically scan resumes looking for a perfect fit—and it is the resumes of specialists rather than generalists that typically offer a perfect fit. Also, consider your personal needs: flexibility, right? You have more leverage to create the work life you want if there aren't five thousand people with the same, broad expertise as you. Develop a special niche for yourself, and then, over time, craft a position in which you give clear value to the company at reduced or rejiggered hours.

The expertise you develop will also give you a step up in the entrepreneurship world. More and more people are starting businesses as a way to create a flexible work life, and the best-odds business is one in an area where you're an expert.

Figure out what your strengths are and hone them. Sure, take varied positions in the company, and learn a range of skills, but make sure people know where your best talents lie. People with power need to see you as someone who is extremely good at something, and no one is extremely good at everything, so don't sell yourself that way to senior managers.

Conclusion

This is one of the most exciting times in the history of work. Never before has work focused so much on fun, personal development, mutual respect, and making the world a better place. I hope the advice in these pages gives you guidance for navigating this exceptional time.

I did not have a guidebook, which made for a lot of moments of feeling lost, doubting myself, and asking people who had never faced my situation to give me advice on my situation. It was not good. I hope this guidebook gives you more self-confidence to get to know yourself, trust your instincts, and align your work with your values. In this way, you can have a fulfilling career without pandering to outdated rules and conventions that undermine fun.

But the rules in this book cut two ways. You don't need to follow someone else's rules about climbing ladders and giving up your personal life. But you do need to follow the new rules of self-discovery. The new workplace is about fulfillment and flexibility, and if you want to get those things in your career, you need to be honest with yourself about who you are and what you want.

Being honest is saying that it's a high priority for you to have a useful and fulfilling career, and that you're willing to put a real amount of energy toward self-discovery. That doesn't mean whining to your friends about your boss. And it doesn't mean taking an aptitude test and then running to the help wanted ads.

Knowing yourself and what you need is a continuous endeavor.

A great career doesn't fall on you. You have to seek it out by moving in the direction toward which your heart pushes. If you know yourself and you take passion seriously, your work will provide structure and support for a happy life.

These new rules for success will guide you through this process. So don't bother with ladder climbing to reach your goals at work and in life. You can succeed on your own terms with a fresh path that doesn't necessarily go straight. And when you feel like you're veering off course, use this book to help you find your way.

Good luck on *your* route to success.

Index

PENELOPE TRUNK is a columnist at Yahoo! Finance and the *Boston Globe*. She founded the blog Brazen Careerist, which has been written about in *TIME* magazine and the *London Observer*. Trunk's syndicated column, also titled Brazen Careerist, has run in more than 100 publications around the world. Web sites that have published Trunk's writing include TIME.com, USATODAY.com, and the *Wall Street Journal*'s CareerJournal.com.

Trunk's prior experience includes more than ten years in the technology and consumer products industries. She has launched new businesses for multinational corporations and founded three of her own companies. Trunk has endured an IPO, a merger, and a bankruptcy. She also played professional beach volleyball.